The Only Complete and Comprehensive Guide to the Creation and Marketing of School Plays

Each year, high schools and junior high schools (and amateur theaters) around the country put on plays. Where do these plays come from? From specialty publishers who are always looking for writers of entertaining three-act comedies and dramas. Not only can you write and sell a play to these publishers, but every time your play is performed, you receive a royalty payment!

Using the guidelines and instructions in this informative book, you too can try your hand at this lucrative market—even if you've never written a play before! Veteran playwright Frank Priore takes you through the mechanics of play staging, with explanations of lighting, sound, and costuming.

Step by step, he shows you how to start with an idea and then go through the process of creating a ready-to-be-produced play.

- **Learn the secret "tricks of the trade"**
- **Detailed and highly successful formulas for writing and developing characters, for stage dialog, for plotting**
- **The extras that mark a script as professional**
- **The best ways to get your work read, bought and produced!**
- **Includes an extensive listing of play publishers' actual guidelines. Read their preferences in their own words!**

"This book is incredible. A real landmark in the field."
— Steven Fendrich, Publisher
Pioneer Drama Service, Inc.

Author Frank Priore

About Frank V. Priore

Frank V. Priore is a veteran of over thirty years in the theatre. A graduate of the New York Academy Of Theatrical Arts, he had a brief career as a professional actor before devoting himself to acting, directing, producing, and writing for the amateur stage. He founded several community theatre troupes within the outer boroughs of New York City.

As a playwright, Frank has had over fifty of his plays published, including three anthologies of chancel drama for young people.

He lives in College Point, New York with his wife, Catherine. His idea of heaven is sitting at the picnic table in his backyard and tapping out the dialog of a new play on the keys of his laptop computer while puffing on an eight inch, 54-ring, handrolled, imported cigar.

Getting Your Acts Together

by Frank V. Priore

An illustrated, comprehensive step-by-step guide to writing, publishing, and selling plays to the School Market. Complete with actual Publishers' guidelines!

Toad Hall Press

Getting Your Acts Together
Frank V. Priore
ISBN: 0-9637498-4-6

Copyright (c) 1997 by Frank V. Priore

Windows and *Windows 95* are trademarks of the Microsoft Corporation

First printing: September 1997

Toad Hall Press

A division of Toad Hall, Inc.
Rural Route 2, Box 16 B
Laceyville, PA 18623

"All theories of what a good play is, or how a good play should be written are futile. A good play is a play which when acted upon the boards makes an audience interested and pleased. A play that fails in this is a bad play."
                                        —Maurice Baring

"The Play's the thing
wherein I'll catch the conscience of
the king."
                                        —William Shakespeare

"It'll play in Peoria."
                                        —John D. Ehrlichman
                                        (Who wasn't talking about the theatre,
                                        but excuses for Watergate!)

Dedication

To the memories of my Dad, who never quite understood what my fascination with "all this acting stuff" was, and my Mom, who did.

Acknowledgments

I wish that I could list the names of all the hundreds, even thousands of people with whom I've worked in amateur theatre productions over the years. In fact, I wish I could remember many of their names! So many different people who are so generous with their time and talents come together for any given production, that it is very hard for anyone to enumerate them. They are all very special people to me, and I love every one of them. And they are all part of this book. Without them, it would have been impossible for me to have been inspired to write for the amateur stage.

I am especially grateful to LaVonne and Ronnie, my other two "musketeers." Together, the three of us have surely had more adventures on the stage than the original musketeers had throughout all of France! And to Bob, Annie, and The Phoenix Players. I love you all! A special thank you to Millie. I often wonder how theatrical troupes who do not have Millie helping their productions ever manage to put on a show!

And where would this book have been without Sharon Jarvis? Surely not in your hands! Perhaps, never even written.

Thanks also to my wife, Catherine, who has put up with twenty-eight years (and counting) of my love affair with the theatre, and has even stage-managed shows for me while carrying our children. Also, Lorraine, who has been proofreading her Pop's stuff almost as long as he's been writing it; Greg, without whom I would not have been able to enjoy the summer sunshine while composing much of this book on a laptop in my back yard; Ginny and Bruce, who had to listen to three months of me saying: "Talk to you later, guys. I've got to work on my book"; Gary, who came to my rescue at the last minute; Leonora, who still insists that her tremendous help is "nothing at all"; and to my grandchildren, Christopher and Margory for...well, just for being Christopher and Margory.

Table of Contents

# Introduction

Why an Amateur Play?

*I*f I can choose to write novels, where the "big" money is, why would I want to write plays for the amateur market?

Because that's where the *steady* money is. A good playwright, one who knows the ins and outs of the amateur market and can produce scripts that are easy for amateurs to produce and entertaining to perform, can quite reasonably expect to sell most, if not all of his or her work. I've been writing plays for this market for more than twenty years, and I have sold every play (over fifty) I have ever written.

Make no mistake—you won't get rich writing plays for amateurs; however, you *will* be able to provide yourself with a steady supplemental income *while* you are turning out scripts and *for a good many years thereafter!* One of the nice little fringe benefits of being a playwright who writes for the amateur market is that royalty payments continue, in many cases, well into your retirement age. Publishers will keep your plays in their catalog for as long as they continue to "earn their keep." If you are able to create scripts that do not quickly date themselves out of consideration for production[1] because of current topical references, your plays could stay in a catalog for twenty years or more.

Royalty statements from every publisher who lists at least one of your plays in his catalog arrive in your mailbox two to four times a year, depending on the individual publisher's reporting cycle. *And they are accompanied by*

---

1. This book will show you how!

checks! Payment is made for each play that has been produced by amateur troupes since your last statement.

The money represents your share (usually 50%) of the royalties paid to your publisher for each production of one of your plays. *Manna from Heaven!* And it descends upon you at regular intervals! High schools, colleges, and other amateur acting troupes go into production year-round. If it's your play they are producing, there's a royalty check headed for your doorstep! In addition, you will also receive a percentage (usually about 5 - 10%) of the sale of the playbooks sold, both for production purposes and as reading copies for prospective productions.

There is an active and constantly growing market for good plays written specifically for amateur use. And you can help supply this market's needs! Everything you need to get started in this lucrative field is contained within the pages of this book. There are chapters devoted to understanding the needs of this market, the technical information you'll need to know about the "mechanics" of theatrical production, the writing of your play and the marketing thereof.

Incidentally, if you're wondering why I have devoted this book to writing for the amateur rather than the professional theatre market, here's why: (a) The professional market is a hard, *extremely hard* market to crack, particularly if you are not already well-known in the entertainment industry, and (b) the needs of this market are slim indeed.

Perhaps thirty or so productions make it to Broadway every season. Of those, virtually all are musical extravaganzas, particularly the sort that rely on glitzy gimmicks such as falling chandeliers or smoke-and-flame-filled ascents to the heavens. This is not, by the way, due to some conspiracy by producers to keep meaningful drama from treading the well-worn boards of The Great White Way. It is, unfortunately, what contemporary theatre-goers, forced to part with upwards of seventy-five dollars a seat, *want* to see for their money. Out-of-town visitors and business executives, who are making up more and more of the Broadway audience of late, simply do not want to tell the folks back home in Podunk that they spent their one night on Broadway attending a stirring production of *Romeo and Juliet*.

Of the few straight plays that manage to squeeze their way into production each year on Broadway, most are revivals of tried-and-true plays from theatre history, or British imports.

Sadly, most will not even return their investors' money.

If you are thinking of shooting for Off-Broadway, you will probably not fare much better there. Plays that run Off-Broadway operate under virtually the same rules as their more prestigious cousins uptown. This means that the cost of mounting these productions is quite high. Producers, who stand to lose a bundle if their offering flops, tend to go with established playwrights who have a proven track record.

There is a market for Off-Off-Broadway plays, but you have to understand that what is known as Off-Off-Broadway covers a broad spectrum of semi-professional and "sort of" professional productions. Most are staged in phone-booth-sized theaters, and are low-budgeted (which means your chances of actually getting paid for your work are remote, at best).

Contrast all of this with the *thousands* of amateur productions that light up the stages of small-town (and even large town!) American high school auditoriums every year.

That's why I prefer to write for a market that consistently provides me with remuneration for the hard work I put into my plays. If you feel likewise: read on, MacDuff! There's gold in them thar footlights!

Chapter One

Understanding Your Market

I f you've chosen to write plays for the amateur market (a wise decision!), a very important first step is to understand the nature and composition of this market. In broadest terms, it is divided into two elements: school productions and community theatre. School productions can be broken down further into: junior high and high school (grouped together) and college. Community theatre presentations generally fall into the categories of either church groups or "little theatre" (also known as "regional theatre").

By "church groups," I am referring to troupes that are composed primarily of members of a particular church congregation. Somewhere along the line, some parishioners decided to heed the oft-repeated Judy Garland/Mickey Rooney movie line: "Hey, let's do a show!" Such groups generally have a small stage that is part of their own church building or a church school auditorium. This stage is usually available to them free of charge, and they are funded (though not to a great extent) by money from the parish coffers.

Community theatre groups are usually autonomous, i.e., not sponsored by any parent church or other organization (other than their own). Virtually all community theatre companies have one or more board or production staff members who have had some past professional or semi-professional experience with dramatic presentations. Many of the actors who perform regularly in community theatre productions are young, aspiring thespians trying to "make it" so that they can give up their day jobs and work in the theatre full time. In order to add to their on-stage experience, they perform with one or more community companies. It is not unusual for them to act in a half-dozen or more productions each year, or to be rehearsing for more than one show at a time.

Community theatre troupes also attract many local performers and backstage workers. Almost all have appeared in high school or church group productions and have a great love of theatre, but have taken on responsibilities, i.e., a family, early in life that prevented them from pursuing a life in the theatre.

So, Who Should I Write For?

I would strongly suggest that you concentrate on the high and junior high school market. In fact, this book is geared toward getting your scripts published in this specific area of the amateur market. Here's why:

The play selection committees of both church and community theatre companies tend to turn toward past Broadway hit plays (the works of Neil Simon, Kaufman and Hart, et al.). The exceptions would be some community troupes that by charter or mutual decision of the board concentrate on producing theatre classics. These may be either contemporary classics (Miller, Williams, O'Neil, Shaw, etc.) or less frequently, well-known material from the *classic* classics (Shakespeare, Goldsmith, Greek tragedies, and such). Either way, they are not looking for new material.

There are some community groups that seek out new material, but in most cases, the payment for its use is minimal, token, or even non-existent. If your goal is merely to see your work produced on the stage, by all means, write for this market. If you're looking to make money, though, this is not the market for you.

Likewise, college or university productions have little to offer as a market for freelance playwrights. While they do use quite a bit of new material, almost all of it is the work of the university's own Drama Department students.

Lest you be discouraged by the news that many areas of the amateur theatre world are not actively seeking your scripts, be assured that the remainder of the market, the high and junior high productions, is the lion's share! There are tens of thousands of American high schools and junior high schools, and most of them produce at least one play a year. This is the market you should be aiming for. It is a rich and substantial selling ground for the playwright who thoroughly understands its needs and can cater to them.

Farce provides a fertile field for a playwright's imagination.

The goal of this book is to help you to create the kind of bright, witty, easy-to-produce plays that will start those royalty checks parading to your mail drop.

The Basic Elements of a High School/ Junior High Play

It was not by accident that I used the word "witty." You will be writing for a market that is driven primarily by comedies.

Fact of Life #1: You will sell twenty-five comedies for every drama you sell

Moreover, *farcical* comedy sells even better than "straight" or strictly joke-driven comedy. Farcical comedy is very light material (no heavy-handed themes here) that has very improbable plot elements and uses characters that are usually larger than life.

Farce provides a fertile field for a playwright's imagination. For example, I began work on one of my more popu-

3

lar farces, "Off With His Head" with the following idea: *What would happen if Queen Victoria, Henry VIII, Cleopatra, Marie Antoinette and King Solomon should meet up with each other?* This idea, incidentally, developed from a few lines of dialogue racing around in my head, as explained in Chapter Three. Now, right off the bat, I have most of the elements I need for a good farce: (a) an improbable situation, as each is from a time period widely separated from the others, and (b) characters who even in real life were larger than life! (If you want to find out just how I managed to get them all together or why, you'll just have to buy a copy of the play. Sorry. I just love getting those checks for my percentage of the sales of my scripts!)

A category of farce known as the "Drawing Room Comedy" is particularly amenable to amateur[1] production. This type of farce, popularized by our British cousins, typically takes place entirely within the confines of a drawing room (a room for receiving or entertaining guests; what we would most likely call a living room today). In the strictest sense, British Drawing Room Comedy is a bit too broad and overdone for modern audiences; however, the concept of writing a humorous script that could be acted out completely in a living room is one that is ideal for amateur production.

A living room is always an easy-to-build set (a prime consideration for this market!). Further, it can be easily furnished. The pieces of furniture (sofas, easy chairs, end tables, etc.) that are needed for such a set are readily available for acquisition or loan. I suspect that most every household in America has pieces of living room furniture stored away somewhere in the attic. It's old, it's out of date, it'll never be used again, but it's *too good to throw out!* "You need it for your show? Sure. Take it. I always knew it would come in handy someday!"

Since the living room is generally the center of, well...*living* in the modern home, it would be quite believable for the entire action of a play to occur there, much more

---

1. For the remainder of this book, when I mention "amateur" production, it will be specifically high school and junior high school production I am referring to.

likely than, say, a bedroom. Actually, you will never be writing an amateur play that takes place in a bedroom.

Fact of Life #2: Amateur material is strictly
"G" rated material.

For the most part, you can't even get away with an occasional "hell" or "damn" in an amateur play. This may seem somewhat strange to you, particularly in an age when movies have scripts composed of about thirty percent filthy dialogue and another ten percent *incredibly* filthy dialogue. (This from an industry that once had such a strict code of acceptable conduct that married couples' bedrooms had to have twin beds!) You may have written a brilliant script, but if it has overt sexuality in it or is peppered with four-letter words, it will not—*not*—sell to the amateur market. Trust me on this.

One of the more attractive elements of a drawing room comedy, as viewed by the play selection committees for amateur productions, is that it is a *single set show.*

Fact of Life #3: A single-set show is much easier
to sell that a multi-set show.

Amateur productions are almost universally low-budget operations. Most of the time, funds available for student activities must be divided up among several different student endeavors. The annual play must compete with athletic programs, the school band, the math club, etc. for available funds. If you have ever been associated with the after-school activities at your local high school, you already know that "available funds" usually are not *very* available!

Advanced algebra is not necessary to figure out that the sets for a two-set show will cost twice as much to built as those needed for a single-set play. This definitely is one area where bigger is not necessarily better.

One area of amateur script writing where bigger is better is, surprisingly enough, cast size. While a show with only a few parts in it is easy to cast, it will seldom be selected as the vehicle for amateur production.

High school drama programs try to be as inclusive as possible. When casting notices for the school show go up, dozens of aspiring actors and actresses turn up to try out. Directors hate to send any students eager to participate in the show packing, so they try to select a play that can fit in everyone who wants to be a part of the production. Along with the 10-12 principal players your script should have, it needs to include *several* smaller roles. Bit parts and even walk-ons are very desirable. Students with *all* levels of talent (including *none*!) will be trying out. If your show has room for all of them, it has a much greater chance of being chosen.

A further understanding of the demographics of school try-out will help you even more in your quest for publication in this market. High school girls tend to be more star-struck than their male counterparts. Twice as many lasses as lads as will turn out for the annual school play. Ideally, your play should have about 25-30 roles available, with a 65%-35% female/male cast mix. There should be at least eight major roles, with no more than twelve. The remainder of the roles should be the aforementioned bitparts and walk-ons.

Some of the smaller parts should also be capable of being "doubled," that is, played by a performer who has appeared elsewhere in the play in another role. This is a big help for a director who does not have quite the expected turnout for the play or has to contend with the inevitable drop-outs that occur along the road to production

Fact of Life #4: The more flexible your play is,
the more likely it is to be sold.

Further, the play's flexibility is not limited to cast composition. We have already gone over the advantages of a single easy-to-build set. Make sure that it is also easy to *furnish*. Don't make the action of the play dependent upon there being a moose head hanging on the wall (they're not as easy to come by as Hollywood movies would have you believe!) Likewise, it is fine to call for a piano on-stage, but don't *require* it to be a *grand* piano. Besides being not nearly as available as an upright, a grand piano is a stage manager's nightmare, particularly within the confines of a high school auditorium stage.

Another area where flexibility is vital is in costuming. I try, whenever possible, to use contemporary costuming in my plays. It is fine to have one or two specialty costumes, such as military uniforms or police uniforms, but avoid creating a play that *requires* period costuming. Most school play budgets can squeeze in a rented costume or two, but cannot afford to rent for the entire cast. Mothers of the students often help out in this area by sewing the necessary costumes; however, asking them to outfit twenty-five or so characters in period costumes can become burdensome.

Finally, this is a market where most of the productions

> Amateur productions are almost universally low-budget operations.

will be acted by people new to the stage. (Most actors and actresses have had their first exposure to the theatre on a high school stage.) This must be taken into consideration when writing dialog. Long, drawn-out speeches may be easy for experienced actors to handle, but stage neophytes will (a) have a hard time learning them, and (b) rush through the speeches on-stage just to be done with them. Either situation will hinder a good performance of your play.

Each of the areas mentioned above will be dealt with in more detail in further chapters. For now, just remember that the easier you make your play for the actors to perform, for the director to direct, for the set designer to build scenery for and furnish, and for the producer to finance, the more amenable a publisher will be to considering it as an addition to his catalog.

Chapter Two

Technical Information You Need To Know About The Stage

Before you begin to create scripts for the amateur play market, there is some basic information about that microcosmic universe known as the stage that you need to know.

Stage Geometry

The four points of the compass give us a convenient frame of reference that enables us to get from one place on the map to another. Nebraska is *north* of Kansas, for example; Oklahoma, south. The stage itself has a clearly defined and universally accepted frame of reference, a "roadmap," if you will, that enables the playwright to indicate movement and precise positioning on-stage. Since you are going to be creating scripts for the stage, you need to know how that roadmap is organized.

I'm sure you've seen numerous cartoons in which characters about to beat a hasty retreat from their pursuers say as an aside to the audience: "Exit, stage right" or "Exit, stage left." Unless you've already done some theatrical work, you might wonder if there any difference between "Stage Right" and just ordinary "right." Yes, there is—and it's a very important difference. Stage Right is defined as

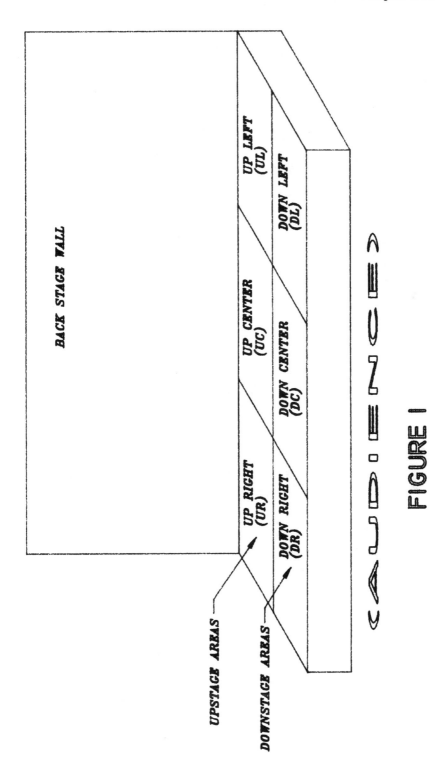

FIGURE I

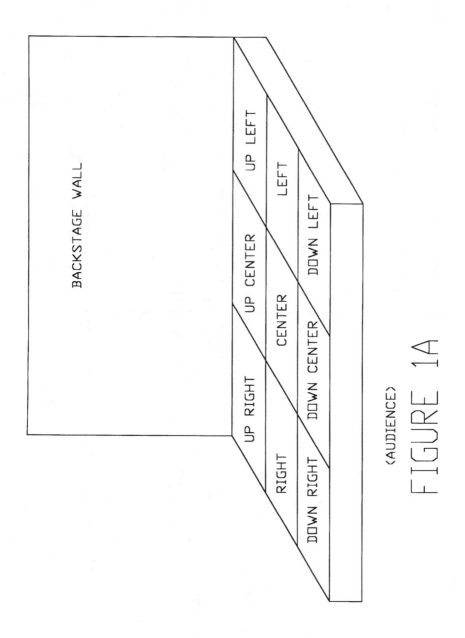

BACKSTAGE WALL

UP RIGHT	UP CENTER	UP LEFT
RIGHT	CENTER	LEFT
DOWN RIGHT	DOWN CENTER	DOWN LEFT

‹AUDIENCE›

FIGURE 1A

the side of the stage on an actor's right *when he is facing the audience.* Likewise, Stage Left is the area on his left side as he faces the audience. The middle area of the stage is called, logically enough, "Center."

For a playwright's purposes (I'll explain what I mean by that shortly), the stage is further divided as follows: Picture a three by two grid superimposed upon the stage, dividing it into six distinct areas (See Figure 1). The right side (Stage Right) is subdivided into two areas: Up Right (abbreviated UR), which is the right side box farthest from the audience, and Down Right (abbreviated DR), which is the right side box closest to the audience. The left side (Stage Left) is similarly organized into the areas Up Left (UL) and Down Left (DL). The two center areas are Up Center (UC) and Down Center (DC).

This six-area grid used by playwrights differs somewhat from the standard stage divisions used by directors when blocking the actual movement of actors on-stage. For their purposes a three-by-three, nine area grid is employed (See Figure 1A). This grid enables the director to place actors more precisely than a six-area grid would. This nine-area grid takes "territory" away from the other six blocks to create three additional areas in the middle of the stage. These areas are designated Left (L), Center (C), and Right (R). What this does is sub-divide the Left, Center and Right thirds of the stage into three, rather than two areas each.

While the standard nine-area grid is quite helpful to the director once a play is actually in production, the degree of precision in character placement which use of this grid permits may actually be an encumbrance to the playwright. As will be explained in later chapters, a good rule-of-thumb for playwrights is: the fewer stage directions that appear in a script, the better. Use of the six-area grid allows the playwright to indicate about where an actor should be at times when that actor's placement serves an important purpose in the script, without micro-managing the play and tying the director's hands by insisting that an actor be placed in a precise position at that point. For example, if an actor is about to employ an "aside" (See Chapter Ten), it is easier to accomplish this from a downstage position than from an up-stage location, but it doesn't really matter from the stand-point of the script itself precisely where downstage that actor is placed. The exact placement for any individual production will be up to the director (as it should be!).

At this point, you may be asking yourself what all this "up" and "down" business is. Simply stated, the half of the stage farthest from the audience is known as the *up-stage* area, while the half of the stage closest to the audience is the *downstage* area.

These designations are not arbitrary, by the way. Nowadays, all theaters, whether intended for the presentation of live performances (known as "legitimate theatre," incidentally) or for the screening of movies, have the rows of audience seating set into a floor that slopes downward toward the stage or screen. This is, of course, for ease of viewing by all members of the audience. There was a time, however, during the early days of the theatre, when the floors of theaters were level and it was *the stage itself* that was sloped (or *raked* in theatre jargon). The area of the stage against the back wall was higher than the area closest to the audience. This was also done for the purpose of making the action on the entire stage easier to see for the audience. So, when an actor was moving toward the back of the stage, he was actually moving *up* the stage (upstage), and when he was moving toward the audience, he was moving *down* the stage (downstage).

I'm sure you've heard the term "upstaging" used often in reference to someone stealing someone's thunder by their actions, as in: "Her lavish gown and flashy entrance completely *upstaged* the hostess of the party." The word has its origin in the division of the theatrical stage into "upstage and downstage." As applied to actual conduct on-stage, an actor is said to be upstaging another when he moves himself into a position far upstage of another actor whose dialogue requires him to speak to the first actor. In order to deliver his lines to the actor upstage of him, he is forced to turn his head upstage (and away from the audience). One of the "golden rules" of acting is that you *never*

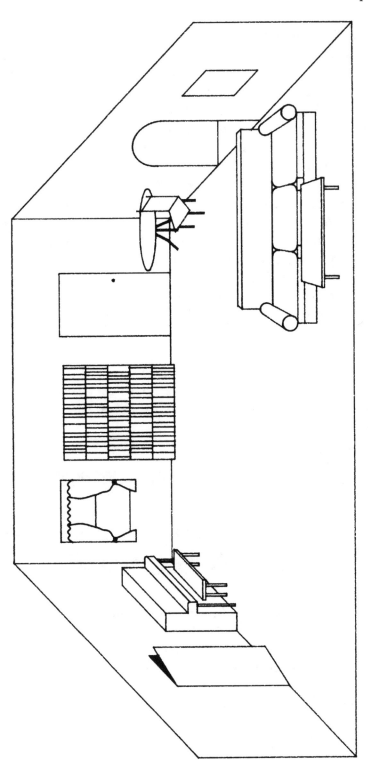

FIGURE 2
A BASIC ONE-ROOM INTERIOR SET

turn your face away from the audience to deliver a line.

Intentionally "upstaging" another actor is considered most unprofessional. If the director or producer becomes aware of it happening, you can rest assured that an understudy will be performing that role for the rest of the run of the show. In later chapters, we will deal with not creating situations which would force one character to upstage another.

An actor who moves upstage to get around another on-stage actor or piece of furniture is said to be moving *above* that actor or piece of the set. A similar move downstage would be moving *below* same. On the sloped stages of antiquity, he actually *would* be moving above or below another actor or a piece of the set.

The other directions involving movement by actors are self-evident. An actor could Enter, Exit, Cross, Rise, Sit, etc.

The "Power" of Stage Positions

Some positions on-stage are "stronger" than others; that is, lines spoken from certain areas of the stage are more likely to be effective in bringing across a message or emotion to the audience. This is not any sort of acoustic phenomenon, by the way. It is, rather, a psychological effect.

> Intentionally "upstaging" another actor is considered most unprofessional.

The strongest position on-stage (using the standard nine-area grid) is the Down Right area. The Down Left area is considered almost as strong. Heavy dramatic moments are usually played in one of these areas, and key lines are likely to be spoken from them.

Another strong area is Up Center. When an actor speaks from that area he is said to be "taking the stage," as all attention will be diverted to him.

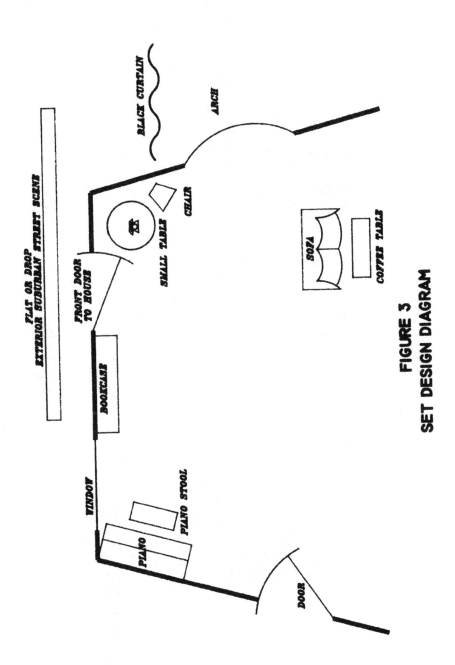

FIGURE 3
SET DESIGN DIAGRAM

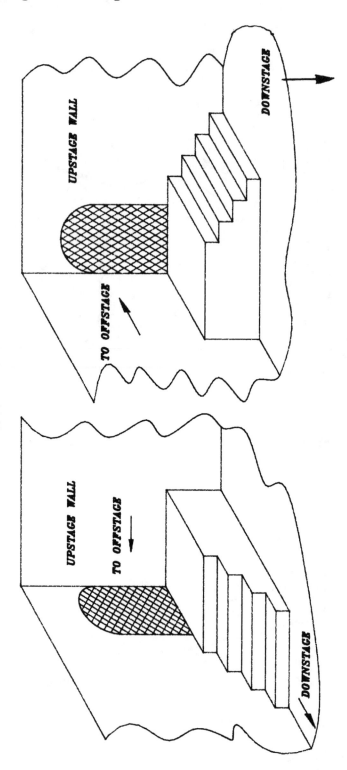

FIGURE 4

The "ordinary" action of the play tends to take place in the Left, Right, Center, and Down Center areas of the stage.

The two weakest areas are Up Right and Up Left. Nothing terribly important is usually played or spoken from these areas as a rule.

The above is supplied for informational purposes only, to help you to better understand the dynamics of what is going on on-stage during the performance of a play. By no means should your script attempt to call for actors to be in a specific area because of your perceptions of the relative "worth" of particular dialog. Once again, that is the director's job.

Sets

The walls, as well as the doors, doorways, and other means of entrance to and egress from the stage in a standard interior set for a single room on-stage, would be organized similar to those in an ordinary room, but there are some very important distinctions between a stage set for a room and an actual room in your house. Figure 2 shows a very basic set. Note that the left and right walls are *angled* from somewhere near the extreme DR and DL positions toward the upstage wall. If they were at right angles to the upstage wall, the sight lines would make it impossible for audience members seated on the left and right sides to see significant portions of the stage.

Also, furniture is placed so as to give the actors plenty of room to move about without being hidden by pieces of the set. For example, the piano shown in the UR corner would not be placed in the center of the stage (unless it was up against the upstage wall), as doing so would hide any actor who moved behind it.

Doorways (such as the arch shown on the Left wall), as opposed to actual doors, would require a black curtain (or other masking device) to keep the audience from seeing the backstage area. Likewise, doors along the side walls of the set which open in such a manner that a portion of the audience could see the backstage area would have to have some

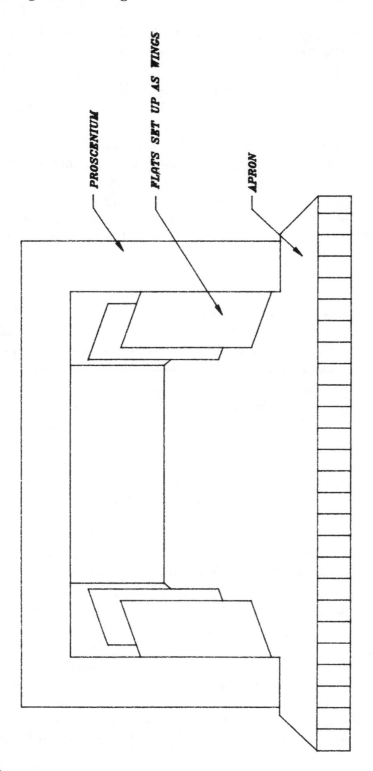

PROSCENIUM

FLATS SET UP AS WINGS

APRON

FIGURE 5

masking device behind them. Of course, any door on the up-stage wall would require a painted flat behind it because whether it opens in or out, members of the audience will be able to see whatever is behind it. The flat or drop (see glossary in the appendix of this book) would be painted with a wallpaper design or some similar indoor background if the door opened to another section of the house. If it was a door that opened to the outside, an exterior scene would be painted on it.

Likewise, if the window shown had holes cut into the flat where glass would be in an actual window[1], rather than being merely a window that was painted on the upstage wall of the set, a flat or drop would be required behind it unless the curtains completely covered the "glass" area and those curtains would never be required to be parted by an actor during the course of the play.

Figure 3 shows a *stage diagram* of the same set. A stage diagram, rather than a realistic drawing of the set (such as that of Figure 2), is what you would include with the manuscript of your play.

Make a point of always including a stage diagram with the manuscript of any script. Doing so, instead of merely describing the set within the body of the text, adds a very professional touch and will help sell your play. All acting-editions of plays include a stage diagram. If you don't provide it, the publisher would have to pay somebody to generate it. Nobody, publishers included, likes to spend more than is necessary for any given project. Additionally, since the set diagram is a necessary part of the printed play script, you may find that the publisher will pass the cost of having a set diagram generated along to authors who do not include same with their submissions.

Occasionally a playwright might call for a set that makes use of *risers* (platforms). A room that is split-level, for instance, would require the use of risers. If your script has the need to make use of risers, make sure you

1. Real glass windows are seldom used in the sets created for amateur shows. Expense, ease of construction (it is much easier to paint a window onto a flat than to install an actual window), and safety are the governing factors here.

do not require them to be too high. A set that allows actors to step conveniently from one level to the other is the best kind of split-level set. If steps are required, you have restricted movement to and from the higher level to those steps. Logjams could occur if several actors must move from one level to another at the same time. Also, don't call for more than one, or at most two, steps. Sets with higher levels are very awkward to work with. Remember, a publisher is looking for plays that are easy to produce. Use of levels, particularly high levels, makes a play harder to perform in or direct.

Frequently, it's important for the audience to know that a second story exists within the house that the play is set in. This second story is, of course, offstage; however, if it is necessary for actors to exit to or enter from that second story, a stairway is needed. Obviously, an entire flight of stairs is out of the question. Most, if not all, school auditoriums do not have stages that have enough height off the stage floor to accommodate this.

The stairway should consist of three or four steps leading to a landing that subsequently leads offstage. The audience will then create in their own minds (even though they don't realize they are doing so!) the remainder of the flight of stairs (the portion that would continue up from the landing). You would call for your steps to be in an upstage corner so as not to block the area behind them from audience view, effectively eliminating it as workable stage space. Steps can either face the audience or be perpendicular to it (See Figure 4).

An important consideration when designing a stage set for your play is what is known as the *fourth wall*. This is the "invisible" wall, the wall of your set that would be between the downstage edge of the stage and the audience if it actually existed. In general, no reference to this wall is ever made by the characters in a play (with the exception of some "experimental" work). It is helpful for you, though, as the playwright, to have in your mind exactly what this wall contains. Obviously, it will never have any doors or other passageways that are used in the course of the play.

While it is seldom done, it is not inconceivable for the play to call for a character to look out a window along this fourth wall or make reference to an object hung on this wall. I wouldn't suggest including such dialog in your play. For the most part, an audience *knows* that a fourth wall to the room must exist, but will forget about it *unless they are reminded that it is there.* A play that *establishes* that the fourth wall is there (by using it [looking out a window] or referring to something on the wall) has now made its audience aware of it for the rest of the performance. It takes a very experienced playwright to write for an audience that has been made aware of the fourth wall. It also takes very talented actors (not most of the high school students you will be writing for!) to work with an established fourth wall.

Most standard stages have a frame or *proscenium* around the downstage edge. The idea is that the audience is viewing a "picture" of life, and all pictures look better within the confines of a frame. Occasionally, the downstage area extends beyond the proscenium. When this occurs, the area forward (downstage) of the proscenium is known as an *apron*. This area is generally rectangular (See Figure 5); however, the aprons on some stages are semi-circular. Try not to require that your play be performed on an aproned stage because many school stages are not so equipped, and once again this is a factor that would limit the flexibility of your script. Write your play so that it can be performed entirely behind the stage's proscenium. (Imaginative directors who have an apron available to them will probably find a way to make use of it, but again, you do not want to require that they do so.)

Figure 5 also shows a set that makes use of wings rather than doors or doorways for entrances and exits. Wings are flats that are angled so as to create entrances to the stage that do not require either a door or a black curtain to mask the offstage area behind them. Feel free to specify a set that utilizes wings rather than continuous walls on the left and right sides of the stage. They are easy to construct (indeed, usually easier than continuous walls), hence will not inhibit the flexibility of your script.

Some sets, though usually not interior sets, call for the use of a cyclorama. This is a large, semicircular, painted drop usually hung in the upstage area. The sides of the cyclorama extend in an arc along the left and right walls of the stage, sometimes stretching all the way to the downstage area. Exterior sets frequently utilize cycloramas to add the effect of depth.

I would not recommend incorporating the use of some of the more exotic theatrical devices such as trap doors or turntables into your set (too expensive for the average high school), or requiring that portions of the scenery be flown (hoisted up into the area above the stage). Also, while many schools perform Peter Pan, I would hesitate to write a script that requires an actor or actors to fly by guy-wire (or any other means). The safety of the for-the-most-part inexperienced actors who will be performing your play would dictate this. Further, in the litigious age we live in, any school's insurer would probably prohibit such an activity anyway, and publishers are well aware of this.

So, now that you've had the ten-cent tour of the stage, let's get down to the business of writing your play!

Chapter Three

The Idea

All writers will agree that the question most often put to them by the public is: "Where do you get your ideas?" As you will find out (if indeed you haven't already), this is the one question a writer is least likely to be able to answer with any degree of accuracy. Some authors, usually those who are tired of being asked, have come up with rather novel responses, which I won't bother to go into here. Suffice it to say that my own stock response has always been: "I get most of my ideas while I'm using the bathroom." While this is not necessarily true (granted, I *have* had some dillys while so situated), it usually stops that particular line of questioning abruptly.

Ideas can come to a writer at any time and in any place. While sitting, standing, walking, or riding the bus, while eating, drinking, sleeping, or even in the middle of a conversation. Strangely enough, for most writers, the place they are least likely to be when the first wisp of an idea comes upon them is at their desk staring at a blank piece of paper in the typewriter (or nowadays, staring at the blinking curser on an otherwise empty monitor screen). In short, it's hard to be creative *when you are deliberately trying to!*

The trick is to be able to recognize a workable idea,

even if it is merely the glimmer of one, whenever and wherever it comes to you. That's why you, as an author, should never be without a pad and pencil within easy reach. If you're a confirmed member of the electronic age, you might, as an alternative, keep a pocket recorder handy for just such a purpose. This is not a bad idea, by the way, although you may get some odd glances from the general public, if you start speaking into your recorder while riding an elevator or waiting on line to pay for your groceries.

What, however, constitutes a workable idea for a play, as opposed to an idea that should be developed into a short story or novel? Obviously, epic-scale projects will not cut it on the stage. *War and Peace* or *Gone with the Wind* are classic novels, but I daresay they would have had a stage audience yawning if played out in their entirety. If some ambitious playwright attempted to squeeze either into a single evening's entertainment on-stage, I have no doubt that it would have to be abridged beyond the point of recognition.

Your task as a playwright is to come up with an idea that will enthrall, delight, and above all entertain an audience in the hour-and-a-half to two hours, playing time allotted to you within the scope of a three-act play. If you are writing a one-act play, you're usually limited to under an hour.

Incidentally, while it might seem logical to begin your career as a playwright by writing one-act plays and then work your way up to a three-acter, you should be aware of two things: (1) three-act plays are much easier to sell to the amateur market than are one-act plays, and (2) in many ways, one-act plays are actually *harder* to write than three-act plays! This book will, consequently, first teach to you work in the three-act format, and then will devote a chapter to the application of these principles to the one-act format.

There are several jumping off points for the central idea of a play. In my own experience, I have begun with something as simple as a snippet of dialog. For instance, the idea for the play I mentioned in Chapter One, *Off With His Head*, germinated from that simple regal pronouncement: "Off with his head!" I had been thinking about what a couple of pig-headed, despotic monarchs might say to each other in the heat of an argument.

"Off with your head!" one might have been likely to have screamed, a la the Queen of Hearts from *Alice In Wonderland*.

To which the other might have responded: "Off with *my* head? Off with *your* head!"

At that point my thoughts, for some strange reason, wandered off into ancient Israel and brought the decidedly non-despotic and legendarily wise King Solomon into the "discussion." I figured he might have offered this bit of sage advice to his regal peers: "No, no. You two have it all wrong. You don't cut off the head; you divide it down the middle!"

Voila! I had an idea around which to create a play. Of course, an entire plot had to be weaved and several other characters brought into the picture. For starters, I had to figure out which kings and/or queens I would gather together, and more importantly *how* I would get them together. My task was complicated by the fact that the monarchs I settled on were from four different countries and *five* different eras. While this presented an interesting challenge to me, I knew I had a workable idea. These three lines of dialog provided me with that "jumping off point" I needed. And, as you will discover[1], once a playwright has a workable idea and knows the mechanics of play creation, everything else will fall into place.

As we've just seen, an amusing bit of dialog could very well become the spark of an idea—one that can lead to the creation of an entire play. Moreover, it doesn't even have to be dialog you have thought up yourself. (You do listen in to what people around you are saying while you're riding on a bus, train or plane, don't you? If you don't, as a writer, you should. Life and the cast and crew of folks who

---

1. By the time you finish reading this book, you will be well acquainted with the mechanics of playwriting and with some tried-and-true methods for finding workable play ideas. I'm afraid you'll have to come up with the actual ideas for your plays on your own. Sorry.

live it generate more honest-to-goodness laugh lines than any comedy writer.) By the way, when I say that you don't necessarily have to think up every line of dialog yourself, I don't mean to imply that you should "borrow" material from other people's written or performed words. Nobody likes being sued.

Be aware that not just any bit of amusing dialog will do. A key concept to remember here is this: it should be *unusual* —something out of the ordinary. In fact, in the creation of comedy for use on the amateur stage, often the farther out of the ordinary it is, the more likely it will develop into a workable idea.

For example, one person's amusing antics as he or she tries to cope with a bothersome neighbor might become the basis of a humorous short story, but trying to make a three-act comedy from such a situation would be pushing it. What if that neighbor happened to be an alien from the planet Gamma XII? Now we're talking play.

Likewise, if you should see your former spouse wander in unannounced through your patio door, you might be surprised as well as either pleased or annoyed (depending upon your past history with that person), but such circumstances would not be likely to become the basis of a play. But suppose your spouse happened to have died several years ago, and it was not actually her, but rather her ghost that decided to pay you a visit? And suppose further that you were the only person who could see or hear her. Do you think you could turn that idea into a three-act comedy? Sir Noel Coward did. The play is *Blithe Spirit*, and it is among his best and is probably the most well-known of his works.

Visitors from the spirit world don't come floating in through our patio doors every day, and I daresay, very few of our neighbors have extraterrestrial origins (though I have my suspicions about some of mine!). To be "unusual," your idea does not necessarily have to have a supernatural or science-fiction element to it. The reaction by one person or several people to a decidedly non-supernatural event can become unusual.

Someone breaking into your house in the middle of the

night would certainly be an unusual event (unless you happen to live in New York City, as I do!). Now, in most cases, this would hardly seem to be the basis of a comedy. Suppose, however, that that person wasn't intent on committing burglary or doing harm to anyone within the house, but was merely fleeing pursuit. If that pursuit was by police or other law enforcement personnel, the event still wouldn't lend itself to comedy. What if it was not police who was on the trail of our fugitive, but rather an entire army. Now, there's some material to work with! George Bernard Shaw built a brilliantly orchestrated comedy around just such a situation. His *Arms and the Man* is one of the staples of both community and professional theatre companies worldwide, even though this play is over one hundred years old!

Possibilities move quickly from the rational to the absurd.

Some other unusual events that have been used successfully on-stage or, in some cases, onscreen include things such as separation of twins at an early age (Shakespeare's *Comedy of Errors* or the film *The Parent Trap*), confused identities (Wilde's *The Importance of Being Earnest*, Goldsmith's *She Stoops to Conquer*), and the old standby of romantic intrigue that farcically escalates (Sheridan's *The School for Scandal*, Wilder's *The Matchmaker*). The playwright Peter Shaffer took a not-so-unusual event, a power blackout in the middle of a party, and through some brilliant writing (and the trick of substituting light for darkness and vice-versa) turned it into an unusual happening in his play *Black Comedy*. One of the oldest known English language comedies, *Gammer Gurton's Needle* (it was first performed in 1566), began with a decidedly normal event, to wit: the loss of a sewing needle, and through an interesting series of farcical twists turned the usual into the unusual and earned its place in the annals of theatrical comedy.

The "unusual" element of your idea does not always

have to be an event. One or more unusual characters reacting to normal events can also lend itself to comedy. What would constitute an unusual character? I will go into greater detail in the chapter about characters; however, we can touch on the subject briefly here.

Eccentricity is an obvious trait that the writer of humorous dialog could exploit. Another would be an exceptionally high or low IQ. I should mention that if your character has an unusually low IQ, it would have to have an origin other than physical. There is nothing funny about people who suffer from mental retardation or illness. Indeed, trying to find something funny about such conditions would be decidedly offensive. If, on the other hand, your character is essentially clueless due to his own choice or laziness, such as the characters Archie Bunker or Homer Simpson, you're on safe ground.

In most cases, the traits of "unusual" characters are exaggerated by the playwright. Exaggeration, as most humorists know, is one of the keys to comedy. Neil Simon, for instance, took the character traits of neatness and sloppiness to extremes and gave us Felix and Oscar, the protagonists of *The Odd Couple*. In case you weren't aware, *The Odd Couple* was an enormously successful Broadway play before it was adapted for the television show that brought it universal recognition and set standards for excellence in TV comedy.

You may have noticed that I have used the words "what if" more than once in describing the thought process that can lead to an idea for a play. As any writer of science fiction will tell you, these are two very important words to an author looking for something truly unusual to write about. Indeed, for many years, one of the better-known science-fiction magazines was entitled: *Worlds of If*.

These are the very words that can also help you turn ordinary ideas into extra-ordinary, that is to say, "unusual" ideas that you can build plays around. "What if" that neighbor was an alien? "What if" a ghost walked through your door? "What if" someone found a time machine hidden in the basement? Or instead of a time machine, "what if" it was the original manuscript of *Hamlet*, or a chest of pirate treasure, or the fountain of youth. As you can see, the possibilities are endless.

When I have finished writing (and rewriting!) whatever play I had been currently been working on, and it is safely on its way to the first publisher on my list (the entire process of manuscript preparation, mailing, which publishers to submit to, etc. is described in later chapters), I am ready to once again begin the process of creating a new play. This process, of course, begins with the unearthing of a workable idea. I say unearthing because that is exactly what I do. (Not literally, mind you. I don't keep a box filled with ideas buried in my backyard!)

Where I go "digging" is in my "idea file," a large, expansion-type manila folder that I keep in the bottom drawer of one of my file cabinets. This is where I store those scraps of paper, torn from the little notebook I always carry with me, upon which I have recorded things that have struck my fancy as a writer as I go through the day-to-day process of existing on the planet. For the most part, these are not terribly unusual things in themselves, but something about them has inspired me to record them for possible future use.

One piece of paper might contain the description of someone who had sat opposite me on the subway. Something about him or her had caught my eye. Perhaps it had to do with the clothes they were wearing—a fellow wearing a very conservative button-down white shirt and tie and a pair of dirty, ripped jeans, a woman dressed in a bright orange blouse and a green plaid skirt, a child not only wearing socks that didn't match, but also sneakers that didn't match. Perhaps someone had an interesting tattoo, or had one located on an interesting portion of his anatomy, like his cheek.

Another paper scrap might contain my impressions of a parade or an outdoor concert or a wedding I attended. A third, a description of a street vendor who used an unusual pitch-line to lure customers in. Yet another would have one of those snippets of amusing dialog I've overheard. In a similar manner, interesting ideas from dreams I've had get recorded, as do bits of dialog that pop into my head, like the aforementioned lines that began with: "Off with his head!"

I retrieve about four or five of these scraps at random. What I then do is take a pad of lined paper, and recopy them — one to a page—onto the pad. I skip a line on each page and then write: "What if...?" on the following line. This is where I let my imagination kick in and lead me where it will.

I begin to list all sorts of alternative existences for characters, if indeed a scrap of paper yielded a character profile. If I have the description of an event or even an observation I had made copied onto a page, I try to add various "What if..." elements that would change it from a relatively normal event (I say "relatively" because something out of the ordinary, no matter how slight, caused me to record it in the first place.) into an "unusual" event.

Not every idea will work as a play, even with all the "what ifing" I can muster. But usually at least one of the five will. If none does, I grab another five and start all over again.

Let me give you an example of how I work on each idea. Let's take the fellow in the button-down shirt and dirty, ripped jeans, for instance. The obvious place to start is by asking myself why he was so attired. My page for this might look something like this:

What if...
    ...he was making a fashion statement?
    ...he was trying to start a fad?
    ...he angered his wife, and she cut all his dress pants in half that morning?
    ...he was going to an interview for a job he really didn't want to get,but needed to report to to keep the Unemployment Office happy?
    ...he made a rude remark to someone in the elevator, and that person was a wizard?...or a witch?
    ...he was an alien spy, and he didn't study his recordings of normal earthling clothing too carefully?

As you can see, the possibilities move quickly from the rational to the absurd. This is fine, actually. Sometimes a mildly unusual character can become the focus of a play. Other times, you need one who is really "off the wall" to spark your imagination and get the creative juices flowing.

This is not, by the way, actually from my files. I made it up just for the purpose of illustration. However, looking at it, the next to last "what if" (the wizard or witch) would be the one that would have the best chance of succeeding as a play. The others are either too "normal" or in the case of the last idea, too preposterous to work. So that's where I would go into detail on another page (or several other, depending on how things develop).

Continuing my thought process, the elevator would be the first thing to go. Its use would force creation of an additional set that would be used for what would be a short scene. This is an important consideration if you are writing for the amateur stage. As has been mentioned before, our aim is for a single set, which obviously cannot be an elevator. (Just try writing a three-act play set in an elevator; I dare you!)

So, let me put our hero somewhere else. Some ideas come to mind: on a park bench...in his own living room...in his office, perhaps. The park bench I reject out-of-hand. It's possible to set a three act play outdoors, and many successful shows take place entirely outdoors. But, in truth, it is harder to justify the same people showing up regularly over a period of time at the same outdoor location (as they would have to for three acts) than it is for one indoors...and I'm lazy.

His living room would certainly be easier, but in this particular instance his office would appear to be easier still. (I told you I was lazy!) It would have to be a big office; a cubicle wouldn't do for the same reason an elevator wouldn't work. A big office would mean that he was an executive of some kind or perhaps a hot-shot lawyer. A politician is another possibility.

Now, why would a wizard or witch be in his office? If he was a businessman, it could be because he was about to construct a mall or a tract of housing on their sacred meeting place in the woods. I could think of a dozen reasons why a lawyer would tick off a witch, and a hundred reasons why a politician might! In addition, I note that lawyers and politicians are easy to poke fun at, so there would be good joke possibilities there.

Before deciding, I would have to think about what kind of other characters I could bring into the play in each case. Remember our goal of 25-30 characters. For the executive, I have other executives, secretaries and other underlings, the contractors he would be using to develop the land, etc. It seems to be an acceptable mix.

The lawyer would have other lawyers in his firm, and again secretaries and other underlings. The politician would have, in addition to his staff, various constituents and perhaps other politicians. In short, all three have possibilities because I can bring in enough other characters. So, none are yet eliminated.

This is how my second page for this idea would look:

Scratch the elevator — never work in three-act.
Where then?
Possibilities:
    Park bench — Nah, outdoor.
    His living room — maybe
    His office — might be better than living room
        Why does he have an office?
            Executive
            Hot-shot lawyer — good jokes
            Politician — good jokes

Characters for office:
    Executive — other execs, secretaries,
        contractors, etc.
    Hot-shot lawyer — other lawyers, secretaries, etc.
    Politician — staff, constituents, other politicians

At this point, I would start a page for each of the three possibilities, and begin to sketch out plot ideas. We will deal with plotting in another chapter, so I won't go into the details here. Before long, either a workable plot would begin to evolve for one or more of the possibilities or all three would fizzle out. If they do, it's on to the next idea, and I start the process all over again. If more than one seems to be yielding the beginnings of a good plot, I'll go with the best and file the others away. At some future date, I may turn them into plays, too!

My MO for developing ideas is certainly not the only way to go about the task, but if you really don't have a clue as to how to get started, you might try it. It has worked for me for the past twenty years.

One final note on idea generation: avoid (like the plague) controversial subjects and sexual situations. High schools won't buy into either, and neither will publishers. Likewise, a play that features racial or ethnic stereotyping or jokes at the expense of people of any race, religion, or ethnicity will *not* sell.

Chapter Four

Characters

O nce a workable idea for a play has been generated, it would seem that the next logical step would be to out-line a plot for that play. Well, yes and no. Yes, there needs to be a framework for the play's characters to operate within and a direction for them to head towards; however, before that is done, the characters themselves must be created.

In actuality, a broad outline of the eventual plot comes about as a natural outgrowth of the process of generating a workable play idea. The specifics of this plot, the scene-by-scene sketch of the play's action, should wait until the princi-pal characters (at least) have been decided upon. There are two good reasons for this. First, the nature of the characters will dictate the direction the scenes will go in, and second, as the play begins to come to life on paper, some aspects (possi-bly many aspects) of the plot will change. If a playwright tries to force characters to adhere to a detailed plot that was created before they were, *they will rebel!*

Say what? Rebel? Characters *you've* created, and pre-sumably could *uncreate* just as easily? Fictitious people who are a product of your imagination...who exist only in your mind...whose very existence can be extinguished by an act of your will? (Gee, kind of makes you feel like your home should be on Mount Olympus, doesn't it?) But the truth is, yes, characters seemingly begin to take on a life of their own once you've thrown a situation at them and they have had a chance to react to it. By "a life of their own," I mean that the your original concept of the characters will change during the course of the play. Characters "grow" as the script progresses. Additional information about their traits and characteristics come to mind as a result of their being "put through their paces" while the plot of the play develops around them and they respond to it.

A character is like a baby. A baby's life is, at first, a blank slate. But it grows, learns, and develops a unique personality from everything it experiences as it moves through the world. Likewise, your characters, whose initial "life" is dictated by the attributes you assign to them on their character sheets (we'll get to them), will grow, learn, and develop personalities (sometimes very different from the ones they started out with) depending on how they react to the situations you put them in.

An example: Let's say you've created a character who is your "bad guy" (or one of your "bad guys"). Initially you've established him as totally depraved with no redeeming virtues whatsoever. Now, in the course of one scene he has cause to do something that could be interpreted as a "good deed." Perhaps you have him returning a purse snatched by another character even *more* of a villain than he is. Why? Who knows? (Actually, *you* do.) Maybe you have decided that the purse was snatched from a woman who reminded him of his mother. Whatever the reason, you had him on-stage at the time, and for the purpose of your plot it was necessary that the purse be returned. He seemed to you to be right for the job. More importantly, you didn't plan for that to happen (or at least you didn't plan for that particular character to be the one who returned the purse) when you initially sketched out your plot, but as your story grew (and took on a life of its own!), having him do this fit in nicely and helped move your story along.

This is fine. A successful play is a dynamic vehicle, rather than a static story-telling device. But now, your character has changed. He is no longer a complete scoundrel. If, subsequently, you try to have him do something that only a truly bad "bad guy" would do, the lines you have him saying and the actions you have him doing will seem wrong in your mind and will "sound" wrong within the scene. And for a good reason—they now *are* wrong! The "new, improved" character cannot and will not *believably* (a key word here) do what the character you've originally envisioned would. The character has, in effect, "rebelled" in that his words no longer ring true in the context of the play.

Just as any given production of a play is a collaboration between the playwright, the director, and the actors, the writing of a play is a collaboration between the playwright and the characters he or she has created.

> Guide your characters gently within the structure of your play.

And this is as it should be. If the playwright tries to strictly adhere to a rigid plot outline, the result will be stale and have no life. If he or she tries to rigidly control every line spoken and every action taken in the course of your play, the characters will become mere puppets and it will show. Their actions will become very predictable, and no playwright ever wants *that* to happen!

Guide your characters gently within the structure of your play, but let them move freely through it. You'll be pleased with the result, and of even more significance, so will your audience (starting with your prospective publisher).

Types of Characters

The various "awards" programs for stage, screen, and television have come up with (so it seems) infinite sub-categories for performers (leading man, leading lady, supporting man and lady, leading man and lady in a *musical*, etc.). As far as we are concerned, however, all characters in a play fall into two main categories: *principals* and *non-principals*.

Arguably, the non-principals can be divided into *speaking roles* and *walk-ons*, but for the purpose of character creation, all non-principals are essentially minor characters. They add depth to the play, provide motivations for principals' actions in many cases, and are needed to make up the larger cast requirements called for in high school productions. Usually, though, they will not require the kind of in-depth analysis by the playwright that the principals do. Consequently, I will describe the procedures I use for the creation of principal characters.

Essentially, the same process is used for the creation of minor characters, but since they do not have as large a presence in the play as do principals, it is not necessary to go into as great detail when creating them. You can, of course, devote more effort to the creation of one or more of your minor characters if you feel their importance in the play warrants it.

As has been mentioned before, amateur productions will need a healthy stock of non-principals to fill out the cast requirements of between 25-30 roles. They can be friends or neighbors of the principals, town folk, passers-by, salesmen, even policemen if the action of the play so dictates. While you must make sure that you find a way to use them in the course of the play, at this point, you can put them on the back burner.

Remembering that you are working on plays that have something unusual at the core of their central ideas, you will need a *variety* of characters to populate the mini-universes you are creating. Your characters contain both *normal* and *eccentric* characters. Understand that I use the term normal to simply mean "not eccentric." All play characters are to some extent larger than life, so my use of the word "normal" is relative.

The variety is important. A play filled with "normal" characters can be boring. Similarly a play filled with zanies is hard to manage from the viewpoint of the playwright. Some crazy, *unusual* if you will, events and characters are essential; however, *constant* nuttiness going on on-stage is hard, if not impossible, to sustain. You can lose your audience just as easily by subjecting them to non-stop craziness as you can by boring them with three acts worth of the mundane. Even the famed Marx Brothers, probably the finest examples of apparently constant zaniness on the screen, kept their audiences from being bored by too much of a good thing (their antics) by giving them a chance to catch their breath now and then. There were always "normal" characters as love interests or other sub-plot elements mixed in.

In general, the protagonist or protagonists of amateur plays are normal characters. This is not a hard-and-fast rule, by the way, but you may find it easier to work with, at least for your first few plays. Your eccentric characters can have roles just as large as your normals, but don't keep them at the center of your plots. Let them "do their stuff" on the periphery of the central action.

Creating Characters

Now that we've got that settled, let's get down to the "nuts and bolts" aspects of creating your characters. Characters come in all sizes and shapes. Each has a distinct personality. As we have seen, these personalities establish themselves in the course of the play, and the characters seemingly take on a "life" of their own.

In order to develop characters who have the ability to "come to life" on-stage, a good deal of effort on your part has to go into their creation. This is not the place to skimp on your time. Memorable plays are populated by memorable characters, and memorable characters do not just "happen." They are skillfully and thoughtfully created. Here's how:

Naming Characters

You might think your characters' names are irrelevant. They are not! I always take the time to insure that each character's name is just right. It must fit him or her like a well-tailored suit.

Look at some of the character names from classical literature. Would Ebenezer Scrooge have been as effective as the miserly humbugger of Christmas if his name was George Johnson? And suppose Margaret Mitchell had opted for Alice O'Hara or Mary O'Hara as the mistress of Tara? Likewise, suppose Shaw had named his pedantic professor Huckleberry Finn and Mark Twain his rebellious raft-rider Henry Higgins?

On the other hand, while the name selected should fit the character and reflect to some degree his or her traits, it should do so *gently*. Don't hit your audience over the head with your selection of names. You should avoid naming characters as if they were featured players in a morality play or the latest superhero cartoon show. Names like *Purity Trueheart* or *Johnny America* are too obvious to be believable.

Likewise, names that are too "generic" such as *Bob Jones* or *Mary Smith* are just too tame to work most of the time. There are exceptions, of course. For example, in my play *Go, Go, Go, UFO!*, some of my charac-

A "character sheet" is handy to have.

ters are aliens from a planet where almost all the people are named either Smith or Jones (except for the few named John or Jane Doe!). Here, the generic nature of my characters' names is part of the humor; i.e., it serves a *recognizable* purpose in the play.

There are also times when it is not necessary to give your character a last name. Quite often, some, or all of a play's characters can get by with only their first name or title (Grandpa, Uncle Joe, The King, etc.). Here, a random sprinkling of Joes, Bobs, Marys, etc. will work for your normal characters. You should still give less-common names to your eccentrics, though. A rule of thumb for last names: If the last names are never referred to in the text of the play, they are not necessary. Don't, however, structure your play to scrupulously avoid referring to last names just because you don't want to think them up.

Sometimes, last names are absolutely necessary for at least some of the characters, particularly in family-oriented material such as plays written for high school audiences. If your play, for example, is centered around a family, that family and everyone that is part of it should have a last name. That will keep your audience (and the school's play selection committee) from making the inference that the relationships among family members is anything other than traditional.

Try, also, to avoid having characters with names that are phonically similar. Don't have a *Joan* in the same play with a *Jane*, for instance, or a *Bob* and a *Rob*. This could cause confusion for your audience.

If you have trouble thinking of proper names, there are several aids readily available. "What to Name the Baby" books are quite helpful here for the selection of first names. For last names, you might try using the White Pages from some major metropolitan city. You can order the latter, by the way, from your local phone company. There will be a charge (isn't there always?), but nothing you can't fit into your writing budget.

One caveat when using phone books: don't use a real person's entire name, particularly if it is somewhat unusual. Though it's not very likely that that person will see your play or otherwise be aware that you have "appropriated" his or her name, there is always the possibility. As I mentioned before, nobody likes lawsuits.

Creating "Normal" Characters

Most of your principal characters should be of the "normal" type. As explained above, each play needs its eccentrics, but usually one or two will do nicely. If your play has too many, it runs the risk of degenerating into slapstick.

> An excellent way to use an eccentric is in sub-plots.

Normal characters do not have to be (and should not be) dull characters, unless, of course, it is important within the context of your play for one or more characters to *be* dull. Characters who are dull without being intentionally dull will spout dull dialog which can only result in a dull play, something you obviously wish to avoid.

So, how do you keep the ordinary Joes and Janes who will populate the world of your play from becoming dull? One of the most certain ways is to give each a distinct, recognizable personality. You can help define these personalities by assigning traits to each character. Decide a character's likes and dislikes, education or lack of, occupations, hobbies, habits (good and bad), even what he likes to read or if, indeed, he likes to read at all. These are all elements of personality.

If it is necessary for the audience to know about any of these traits, let them (again—*gently*). If not, keep them to yourself, but make sure everything your characters do or say reflects the personality you have created for them. Remember that this personality will evolve as the play moves along, so make sure you stay in tune with it. After a character has been through a scene or two, his or her personality will (or should!) emerge from the lines of your play and almost immediately will start to evolve. Once that happens, your character will "rebel" if you try to impose dialog or action that is, well...out of character.

You can, if you wish, decide things like size, color of hair or eyes, etc. if that will help form the characters in your mind. *Do not*, however, disclose this information in the text of your play unless it is *absolutely* necessary. (By "absolutely necessary" I mean that some major element of your plot depends on it being known.) Every physical trait you print in the text limits the number of people who can play the part. If you, for example, describe the character as blonde, five foot three and a half inches with a pear-shaped face and a tiny nose, a great many people will be excluded from being considered for the role, a condition that will lead to *very* low sales of your script. Remember: flexibility is one of the keys to the writing of plays that sell.

A good device for making each normal character stand out in the audience's mind is to make him or her very good or very bad at something. It could be something very minor like doing crossword puzzles or remembering TV characters' names. It could also be something a little more involved such as gardening, painting or...writing. If you find a way to work this trait into your plot, all the better (don't force, though). If not, a reference in the dialog (gently, gently) here and there will suffice. Also, It might be good for a joke or two, or as a "running gag" (something humorous that is referred to several times [but not too many times!] in the play—see the chapter on comedy).

Don't make this little talent (or lack of) too much a part of your character's personality; otherwise you run the risk of moving him or her into the ranks of your "eccentrics." You just want to establish that there is something special about each of your characters, something that will keeps each distinct from one another in the mind of your audience.

One of the tools that I have always found to be very helpful for the initial definition of my characters is a "character sheet." This is a form that you fill out for each of your principal characters. It should contain everything you know about your character. In addition to vital statistics (age, health, etc.) list all the assigned traits as described above, including what makes him or her special.

A "character sheet" is handy to have when you have to check on something like the exact age of your character. You might think that surely you could recall the age of each of your characters, but remember that the writing of a three-act play is a long process—one the typically takes from three months to a year or longer. Over time, you *will* forget some of these things. It is embarrassing to have a character claim to be thirty-four years old in Act One and thirty-six in Act Two (unless two years pass between acts).

A few caveats on character traits: It is not a good idea to have your characters smoking. As well as being currently at the top of the "politically incorrect" hit list, smoking has always been something that parents do not want their children doing (even if they themselves smoke). They would be outraged if their sons and daughters even playacted at being smokers on-stage. Publishers are quite aware of this; consequently, you should be very aware of it if you expect to sell your scripts to them. In addition, many, if not most, communities have extremely strict laws governing the use of any kind of fire (including lit smoking material) in all areas of a theater or auditorium. This includes the stage. Horrendous theater fires of the past have prompted lawmakers to enact all sorts of prohibitive legislation regarding smoking in theaters.

Two other traits that should also be avoided are drinking and gambling. While I'm sure you've seen some old movies that have featured a lovable old drunk or have poked fun at intoxicated people, you generally don't see that in modern films or television shows. Fortunately, Hollywood finally seems to have gotten the message that there is nothing funny about the shattered families and lives that the disease of alcoholism engenders. Likewise, compulsive gambling has caused its share of misery. You would be wise to avoid these traits in your characters.

Which Characters Should Be "Normal?"

The protagonist or protagonists of amateur plays usually work better as "normals." As we will see when we get to the plotting of your play, the protagonist(s) undergo some sort of change as the action of the play concludes. With an "eccentric," the change would inevitably be the loss of whatever makes him or her an "eccentric." This is generally not desirable. If a character catches the audience's fancy due to his or her eccentricity, that is what you, as the playwright, would like to have the audience remember. I have found it much better to have the people who come to see my plays leave the theater chuckling about my eccentrics than to muse on their transformation from an eccentric to a normal character.

There certainly are exceptions. No one would doubt that Scrooge is an eccentric character (although not a funny one), and his transformation is what *A Christmas Carol* is all about. So, if you think you can turn out work on a par with Dickens, go right ahead and transform your eccentrics. Until you reach Dickensian status, though, you should let the transformations happen to your normals.

Most of your minor characters will also be normals. You can stick in a few eccentrics here. Remember, however, that you have less time to establish the eccentricity of a minor character, so the eccentric trait has to be something that is clearly evident (an excessively nosy neighbor, a "You're in a heap a' trouble, boy" policeman, etc.)

Whenever I make a minor character an eccentric, it's usually for the purpose of a specific joke I would like to work into the play. For example in my play *Son Of "A Christmas Carol"*[1], I created a very, very pushy stage-mother who was unceremoniously ushered out of my Scrooge's office and could be heard ranting offstage. I had Scrooge send Crachit out to calm her down specifically to work in the following:

```
Scrooge: Now, now, just talk to her.  I'm sure
         she'll understand.
Crachit: Talk?  Sir, she seems to be a woman of
         very few words.
         (Scrooge opens the door)
Voice of Children's Mother: (Offstage) KILL!
Crachit:  That's one of them!
```

Creating "Eccentric" Characters

For the most part, eccentrics are easier to create than normals because their eccentric traits form the basis of the characters themselves. These traits are among the first things that I put on their character sheet. Working outward from these traits, it is very easy to add in all the details that will flesh out the characters.

Since you have a general idea of your plot from your "idea creation" sessions, you should try to take advantage of each eccentric's attributes to push your plot along. For example, in my play *Heavy Metal!*, one of my eccentrics is the grandfather of the family. He is a scientist whose experiments invariably go awry and end up blowing up his lab. (In case you are wondering, this always occurs as an offstage sound effect. Remember my warning about having anything that involves fire happening on-stage.) This fact created the motivation for the family to move into the house where the action takes place (he blew up their last house!). It is very

---

1.This play was sub-titled "An Improbable Sequel," and indeed it was. The distinct movements of the ground I felt while writing it were undoubtedly caused by Charles Dickens rolling around in his grave. I don't pretend to be on a par with the old master...yet.

important to the plot that the family live in this particular house (you see, it harbors an alien way-station for interstellar transport—a *very* unusual event, I might add). Also, since having this sort of thing in your house is something you could not fail to notice, it was equally important that they have *just* moved into the house. Indeed, my play opens with the family carrying boxes from the moving van into the new house. The eccentric's antics, established within the opening lines of dialog so that the audience knows what is going on right from the start, have very nicely provided my motivation for the family's move into the house.

PETER: (Moves to BOB) Gee, Dad, moving is hard work.

BOB: I know. That's why I hired movers to do it for us. Unfortunately, your grandfather has commandeered both of them to lug in that overgrown chemistry set of his.

KATHY: (With a hand on her hip) You're not being fair! Daddy has a lot of delicate scientific equipment. It has to be moved with special care.

BOB: I'd like to move it with special delivery—to Timbuktu!

KATHY: Bob Morgan, you know as well as I do that Daddy gave us the money for our down payment. If it wasn't for him, we wouldn't have been able to buy this house.

BOB: If it wasn't for him, we wouldn't have had to buy this house. Those nutty experiments of his got us kicked out of our last three apartments. He darn near blew two of them off the map.

> KATHY: He does get carried away sometimes. He
> really is a brilliant man, you know.
> Look at how effective that
> fumigation gas he developed was.
>
> BOB: Oh yes, the fumigation gas. How
> well I remember that. When he was
> finished, not one single rodent or
> insect was able to live in our
> apartment. Unfortunately, neither
> were people!

In this particular instance, I was not only able to provide motivation for the move into the new house with this dialog, but I also managed to establish Grandpa's eccentricity before he made his first entrance. I have my audience all prepped for him, and I don't have to use any of Grandpa's opening speeches to confirm his status as an eccentric.

Eccentrics can also be used to set up sub-plots and sometimes are added just for fun, i.e., the consequent opportunity for jokes that their antics provide. Their traits are almost always exaggerations. I try to begin creation of an eccentric character by recalling some idiosyncrasy of a person I have known (sometimes it is myself!). Then I start pulling at the edges of this quirk until it is exaggerated to the point where I can exploit it to provide humor in my play.

For example, I am a notorious book accumulator. I say accumulator rather than collector because my stash of books is quite eclectic (and also quite large). I routinely donate[2] several boxes of already read books just to make room for the new ones I am sure to buy. In one of my plays, I created a character whose eccentricity was similar, except that he never got rid of any books and his attic was on the verge of

---

2. I donate my books exclusively to prison libraries, by the way. Most public libraries don't need your donations as badly as do prison libraries. Indeed, I often find entire boxes of books that have obviously been donated (there are no library stamps anywhere on them) at public library sales of used books. Prison libraries, on the other hand, are notoriously underfunded. Any book that goes to a prison library will be greatly appreciated by the librarian and will be read by many, many inmates.

collapsing as a result. (Yes, I used this as part of my plot!)

When I was growing up, I had a neighbor who was an inveterate home handyman. His basement was filled with stacks upon stacks of *Popular Mechanics, Mechanics Illustrated*, and every other handyman magazine published. He had racks of screwdrivers, wrenches, hammers, etc. of every possible size, shape, and configuration. His bins of nails, wood screws, nuts, bolts, and washers were all neatly organized and labelled. This was before the era of power tools otherwise his workshop might have resembled something out of Tim Allen's *Home Improvement* show. This would have been very apropos because as with the character Tim Allen plays, his handyman projects were always disasters. To my knowledge, he never successfully built anything that worked, or if it did, worked the way the plans in the magazines said it would. He tried very hard, I'll grant him that, but some of us are just not cut out to be handymen.

Don't be afraid to take your character's eccentricity out to the nth degree.

He was a natural for an eccentric character. With a little stretching here and there, the character that emerged not only failed to have anything work properly, he built devices that would prove to be outright dangerous to have around the house. If he built a remote control for the garage door, the toaster would pop up when it was activated. His automatic mail-opener mashed the letters into *papier mache*.

Dialog describing these two uses of exaggeration appears elsewhere in this book in the chapter on comedy. You will see how these exaggerated traits can be turned into some good laugh lines.

Don't be afraid to take your character's eccentricity out to the nth degree. Exaggerate it as much as possible. If it becomes evident that you have gone too far (his antics become slapstick, for instance, or go beyond the bounds of believability—an important consideration that will be expanded upon in later chapters), you can always back off.

These are the characters that you will find are the most fun to create. And you *should* have fun. Comedy works the best when it is not forced. If you are having fun creating the character and writing dialog for him or her, your audience will too!

Which Characters Should Be Eccentric?

Eccentric characters work best in the background of the plot. That is, what happens to them as a result of the action of the play by the final curtain should be secondary to that of the protagonist(s). This is not to say that their actions should have no effect on the plot. On the contrary, quite often, it is their antics that *cause* the problems that the plot revolves around. Yet, they remain in the background.

When I use an eccentric to precipitate the "problem" that the other principals must resolve, I usually have a short scene that gets him or her in to do the damage. Then I back the character off. While he or she will appear from time to time throughout the rest of the play, I will not have the character contribute too much to the resolution of the problem. There is the temptation to have him or her return to prominence in the final scene as a kind of *deus ex machina* to wave a magic wand of some kind to resolve the problem, but I consider that cheating. It's too easy, and usually will not allow the protagonists to change or grow as a result of their efforts to solve the problem. That type of resolution will leave your audience "unfulfilled." They will feel like they just watched a very forgettable episode of a sit-com rather than a play.

An excellent way to use an eccentric is in sub-plots. For example, in *Oklahoma!*, Ado Annie, the gal who "Cain't Say No," and Ali Hakim, the Persian peddler, provide subplot fun that helps bring the play to life. If it was merely the story of Curly and Laurie's romance (and the "problem" caused by Jud Fry) without all the hijinks of Ado Annie and Ali Hakim going on ancillary to the main plot, I don't think it would be quite the memorable theatre classic that it has become.

Likewise, your eccentrics can have free rein to "star" in the sub-plots of your plays. You can bring them in all three acts to cavort and get in and out of trouble without impacting too severely on the main plot.

Character Sheets

I have included a typical character sheet below. This is the character sheet that I use. It works well for me. Feel free to utilize it in the creation of your characters. You may want to add to it or modify it so as to customize it for your own needs. You'll notice that I leave a lot of room at the bottom under the heading of "Notes." Remember, as a play begins to take shape, the characters will change. Here's where I keep track of those changes.

Keep in mind that each page of your play is equivalent to a minute to a minute-and-a-half of actual performance time.

CHARACTER SHEET

NAME:_____

TYPE OF CHARACTER: [   ] NORMAL   [   ] ECCENTRIC

GENDER: _____   AGE: _____

EDUCATION: _____

CURRENT OCCUPATION:_____

PREVIOUS OCCUPATION(S):_____
_____

ANY SIGNIFICANT HEALTH PROBLEMS:_____
_____

WHERE BORN:_____

WHERE DID S(HE) GROW UP:_____
_____

WHERE ELSE HAS S(HE) LIVED:_____

WHERE DOES S(HE)
CURRENTLY LIVE:_____

HOW LONG:_____

SIGNIFICANT EVENTS IN CHARACTER'S LIFE:
        MILITARY:_____
        MARRIAGE(S):_____

OTHER:_____
_____

CURRENTLY MARRIED: [   ] YES   [   ] NO

TO WHOM:_____

WHAT DOES (S)HE DO TO RELAX:_____

THINGS (S)HE LIKES_____ WHY: _____
                    _____ WHY: _____
                    _____ WHY: _____

THINGS S(HE) DISLIKES: _____ WHY: _____
                        _____ WHY: _____
                        _____ WHY: _____

(FOR NORMALS)
WHAT IS IT THAT MAKES HIM/HER SPECIAL:
_____

(FOR ECCENTRICS)
PRIMARY TRAIT: _____

SECONDARY TRAITS (IF NECESSARY): _____
_____

NOTES: _____
_____
_____
_____

Chapter Five

The Plot

The first and most important thing you need to know about outlining a plot for your play is that you should not attempt to go into elaborate detail in doing so. As noted in the previous chapter, the plot *will* change as you go through the process of actually writing the dialog. Therefore, what you need at this point is not so much a rigid mold to pour your characters into, as a flexible framework through which they can come to life. Remember Priore's first law of play plotting: *Keep the plot flexible*.

Artistic creation of any kind is dynamic. As you begin sketching your plot out, you might find that the events you have planned for Act One do not quite get you where you want to be in Act Two. If they don't, perhaps it's the Act Two "goal" you were shooting for that needs to be changed rather than the Act One steps leading up to it. A third possibility is that the goal may have to be changed completely (even if it is the central idea!).

You may find yourself plotting a play that is entirely different from the one you started out to write. That's okay! In fact, once you let your characters loose within the framework you have created, you might find that what emerges is something that bears no recognizable resemblance to what you began with. And *that's* okay, too! That's part of the fun of writing a play. Sometimes the playwright doesn't know in which direction his or her creation will go, or even what's going to happen next in it! And here's the best part: when the dust clears, any leftover plot ideas can always be used as the basis of other plays! (I never completely scrap any ideas. Like long dormant seeds, they can sprout and bear fruit at any time.)

If this all sounds a bit disorganized to you, there is a good reason for that: it *is* disorganized! Unless you are setting out to create a script destined to become *literature* (also destined to remain an unpublished manuscript in your file cabinet), with a strict, uncompromising structure, the entire process of turning an idea into a play will be subject to so much change that at times it may seem out of control. Starting out with a plot framework is one way of bringing some sort of order to it all. Even if the eventual product goes off on a tangent you couldn't even conceive of at this point, it needs to have started off somewhere. That somewhere is the plot outline.

Keep the plot flexible.

So, where does one begin? Creating a plot outline for a play is a little like the eating of an Oreo cookie. Some playwrights start with the middle and work toward either end. Others do the beginning and end first and save the middle for last. Then there are those who do it in reverse: finish, middle, and then the start. Of course, some of us do plot in the traditional way—starting with Act One, and proceeding to Acts Two and Three in succession.

In short, there is no set formula for the creation of your plot. As has been touched on earlier, the process of coming up with the unusual event or character that forms the central idea of your play will give you a good jump on your plot. The later depends heavily on the former.

If it is an unusual character, the odds are that you are going to want to introduce him or her in the first act and then let the action revolve around the unusual aspects of that character. If, however, you are starting with an unusual event, it could very well occur in Act Two. (Act Three is for the resolution of the various conflicts and problems created and amplified in Acts One and Two, so it is unlikely that you would want to put it there.) Ideas that have begun with some amusing dialog can see that dialog appear *anywhere* in the script. Sometimes the bit of dialog will turn out to be the perfect lines to ring down your final curtain with.

With all this said, let us take the time to tip our hats to the "classic" formula for the plotting of a play. It goes like this:

> Act One: Get your hero up a tree.
> Act Two: Throw rocks at him.
> Act Three: Get him back down.

There is much to be said for this formula, not the least of which is: It works! And it can work for you, no matter where you begin your plot. Let's take a closer look at the three acts you have to work with.

Act One

The first act has two principal purposes: exposition and presentation of the problem (or the *first* problem) for the protagonist(s).

The first bit of exposition you have to present concerns the needed information about the location (what country, state, city, etc. as well as the specifics of the house the play is set in, if indeed, it is set inside a room of a house). At the time you create your plot framework, you are going to have to decide not only where your play is set, but also what information about the setting is important for your audience to know.

There are two ways to present information about the locale of your play: by a full or partial description under the heading "Setting" in the text of your script, and by way of the dialog. Usually, both are used, rather than one or the other. The reason should be obvious—the members of your audience are not going to have a copy of the playbook with them. It is true that they are very likely to have a printed program sitting on their laps, and information about where the play is set is invariably included in programs. Once in a while, they actually read that part of the program. The rest of the time it is your job to let them know.

Some sets, by their very nature, do not need any further explanation—a cemetery, a park bench, the interior of a general store, etc. Such locations will become evident to the audience as soon as the curtain rises, unless the set designer has done a very poor job or is from some avant-garde or surrealistic school of set designing. If, though, there is something important about the setting that is not evident (*which* cemetery, park, or store) you will have to "help" them along by your dialog. I'll show you how in later chapters.

Incidentally, please note that I have emphasized the word "important." If the specifics of the location are not important to the plot, you are just wasting lines presenting them. For example, if it is necessary to the plot for the audience to know that such and such a person is buried in the cemetery your play is set in, then that is important information. If not, then leave the specifics to the audience's imagination.

Occasionally, it is important to the plot that the audience *not* know something about the set. Your plot may contain a surprise element that involves the location (it looks like an ordinary room; however, by the end of the play it turns out to actually be a room in Hell or perhaps a room on a large space ship, for example). This also must be decided at the plotting stage of your play, because all consequent plot developments depend upon it.

As part of the exposition of the first act, all or most of your principal characters will be introduced. The audience will get to know their names and anything special about them that it is necessary for them to know, as well as each character's relationship to the other characters.

Once again, even though the names of the various characters will be provided in the printed programs, you will still have to let the audience know who is who through your dialog.

Every play contains one or more problems for the protagonist(s) to work their way through. You should plan for the introduction of the problem (or the first problem, if there is more than one) to occur as soon as possible in Act One. I would suggest that you do so within the first ten minutes. This is because audiences, particularly modern audiences who are attuned to television, where this always occurs before the first commercial break, bore very easily. If dialog that is primarily exposition goes on for too long without having something "happen," you will lose your audience. And trust me, once that occurs it is very hard to get them *back* "into" your play.

Simply stated, just be aware that you can, and in most cases *should* introduce your problem before you have finished with all the expositionary elements of the first act. As soon as the audience knows where things are going to happen and to whom, they can be "hit" with the problem. Other details about the character(s) and location can be presented later in the act.

> Act One: Get your
> hero up a tree.

You will also introducing most, if not all, of your eccentric(s) in Act One. You should decide at this stage of the game whether they are going to cause or add to the hero's problem, or if you are going to be using them strictly for sub-plot purposes. If the former, plan on giving them a little more "air-time" in this act than you might otherwise allot. Your audience will have to get to know a little more about them and what makes them tick than if they were being utilized only for your sub-plot. Otherwise their contribution to the problem or their motivation for doing so might not be as clearly understood as it should be.

If you want to use them only as second-bananas, either as players in a sub-plot or in strictly-for-laughs roles, then try to work things out so that their appearances won't detract from the central action. Don't, however, just bring them on for a quick "How do you do." As explained in Chapter Eight, if you don't give your audience a reason to remember a character, they will not, and you will have all sorts of problems when you drag them out again in Acts Two or Three to "do their stuff." If you can't comfortably work their appearances into Act One without a disruption in the plot or general "flow" of the play, then wait. Bring them in during the acts that you are going to use them in.

If you are including a sub-plot (I would not opt for more than one, as you only have an hour and a half to two hours of time to work with), set it up in Act One. Don't, however, devote too much of the act for this. You need the time for all the other things that have to go on.

Finally, you must give your audience a reason to come back to their seats after the first intermission. Your goal at the very end of the first act is to make them want to get back to see what is going to happen next. This is accomplished in a number of ways. One of the best (and easiest to do) is to add an important twist to the plot just before the curtain comes down. I'm talking about doing this within the context of the last few lines or ideally *on* the last line of Act One. This is your basic cliffhanger scenario. It has been used successfully throughout the history of theatrical presentations, and has carried over to filmdom and the world of television. It *will* work for you.

The twist can be something as simple as the entrance of a character. For example, let's say your plot goes something like this: Many years ago, mysterious old Uncle Charley had sent a package to your protagonist with instructions that he was to keep it for him, but not open it. It had been stored away and forgotten, but he came across it while cleaning one day. Curiosity gets the better of our hero, and he opens it only to discover that it contains gold doubloons and jewels. They look like they must have been part of a pirate hoard. Where did Uncle Charley get them? Did he find them or steal them? If they are stolen, then from whom? Should they be turned in to the police? Will Uncle Charley return someday come to claim them? Is he even still alive? (Now this a *problem*, if ever I saw one!)

They have been spread out on the dining room table, as the protagonist tries to figure out what to do about the situation. While he is considering his options, the door opens and in walks —who else?—Uncle Charley. Curtain.

See how it works?

One last word about the end of Act One, which also applies to the end of any act in a comedy. Try (try very hard!) to have the audience laughing as the curtain descends. In the aforementioned example, they will probably laugh at the entrance of Uncle Charley, so additional dialog would not be necessary (other than an exclamation of surprise from your protagonist, such as: "Yipe! Uncle Charley!").

You *can* get your curtain-drop laugh with a line. In fact, at the end of the third act, you almost have to. There's no more play left for you to resolve a plot twist in, unless you employ a "Oh, no, here we go again!" ending (explained below). Since we are concerned with the creation of a plot and not dealing with the writing of dialog at this point, suffice it to say for now that you should plan to have a humorous event happen at the end of each act. If in the actual writing of the play, your event turns out to be not quite as funny as you thought it might, you can punch it up with a snappy laugh line or two.

> Every play contains one or more problems for the protagonist(s) to work their way through.

Act Two

By the time your play has reached the second act, all of the exposition material should be out of the way. The exception to this would be some surprise expositionary element that you have deliberately withheld from the audience in Act One in order to introduce it at an appropriate spot in the second or third act.

In addition, you should have successfully gotten your hero or heroine up the proverbial tree. Now, it's time to throw some rocks!

There are three ways to do this. The first is to complicate the problem. You can add in factors that either change what was a simple problem to a complex one or take a problem that was complicated to start with and make it even *more* complicated. The idea is to so entangle your hero in his or her predicament that the audience will be sent off to the second intermission wondering how he or she is ever going to get out of the mess you got them into.

The second means of "throwing rocks" is to add an additional problem. This one should cause at least as much trouble for the hero as the first. In fact, when the second is added to the first, the whole should be greater than the sum of the parts. That is, while your hero could be reasonably expected to handle one problem or the other, the two should work together, and the aggregate situation should appear to be one that is more than he or she could deal with. By "working together," I mean that some element or elements of one problem should change the other from one that might be easy to solve to genuine dilemma.

As an illustration of this, let's return to old Uncle Charley. Suppose one of the items in his little treasure chest is a statuette of an ancient god. Further, by stealing it, poor Uncle Charley has incurred the wrath of that god, and has had his life made miserable as a result. The only way to rid himself of the god's enmity is to return the statuette to the temple he stole it from.

Unfortunately, Uncle Charley has chosen a most inopportune time to pop in and surprise our hero—just as he is holding the statuette up to examine it. The shock of Uncle Charley's sudden entrance startles him and causes him to drop the statuette. Of course, it shatters into hundreds of unrecognizable fragments.

If he had dropped and broken it without Uncle Charley being on the scene, it would have caused a second problem, but not a big one. *Oh, my. Clumsy me; I busted it. I hope Uncle Charley doesn't notice that it's gone if he ever returns.* But with old Charles there specifically to get the statuette because he needed it to get himself out of *his* predicament, the breakage has caused the plot to get much more complicated.

The final way to add to your protagonist's woes in the second act is to *simultaneously* solve the first problem while adding a second and even more disastrous situation for him to deal with. For this to work, whatever is done by the hero to solve the first should engender the second. In other words, have him climb his way out of the proverbial frying pan only to land right in the fire.

If you include a sub-plot, Act Two is where you will develop it. The best time to do this is in the middle of Act Two. The hero's problem complications should bracket the sub-plot; i.e., you should devote time to them both before and after your work on the sub-plot. The problems of the hero are what should be on the audience's mind during the second intermission, not the sub-plot. While I wouldn't resolve the sub-plot in this act, I would bring it to a point that will enable you to resolve it without too much ado in Act Three.

The second act also gives you an opportunity to flesh out the characters, both normal and eccentric. This should be done in the course of problem complication and sub-plot, not as dialog segments totally unrelated to either. Don't let your character development be so intrusive that it distracts from the plot. Also, don't let the character development cause the play to go off on a tangent. If you do so, you run the risk of making the audience think that you are adding an *additional* plot or sub-plot, and will, in truth, confuse the hell out of them. If you lose your audience during Act Two, it is not just hard to get them back, it is all but impossible!

If, in the actual writing of the play, the characters themselves "want" to go off on a tangent, and you find they are "rebelling" if you force them away from it, you may have to accommodate them. (Remember, they are your collaborators!) If this occurs, you will have to see if you can incorporate the tangent into the plot or sub-plot or whether you will actually have to replace one or the other with it. Either way you will have a lot of re-writing to do, but you may find the end result is a better play than the one you originally envisioned.

Finally, don't forget to close this act on a laugh, just as

you did Act One. At this point, you will be more comfortable with your characters, so it should be easier to get them to produce that required curtain-drop laugh.

Act Three

Act Three is where it all comes together. Problems are resolved, characters are changed for the better or the worse, as the case may be, and everything is tied up neatly before the final curtain. I don't mean to imply that every play should have a happy ending (though you'll do better with ones that do!), just that when the play concludes, there should be no loose threads. If, for example, in Acts One or Two you sent Grandpa out on a blind date with the president of the local Woman's Club, who also happens to be a super-spy for the Republic of Far-off-istan, you're going to have to bring him back from it (accompanied or not) in Act Three so the audience will know how things turned out. (Although, to tell you the truth, I'm not sure I'd want to know.)

The bottom line is this: as the final curtain falls, your audience should not leave the theater feeling confused about one or more parts of your play. Of equal importance to you as a playwright for the amateur market is the reaction high school Drama Department play selection committee members have after reading your script. If anything is left unresolved or even if they are *not sure* whether something is resolved or not, they are not going to recommend your play for production. Remember that you are not writing for an *avant-garde*, artsy corps of theatre-goers who might applaud obfuscation as being "highly interpretive" or "new age." You're creating plays whose audiences are going to be composed, by and large, of the mothers, fathers, friends and neighbors of average high school teens. They want to be *entertained*, and if they are confused by your play, they will not be entertained by it. Write dialog that will make them laugh and create a plot that is easy to follow and resolves itself nicely in Act Three, and you can't go wrong.

A few words need to be said about the ending of your play. As I have mentioned above, you should have the curtain descend on a laugh. However, the third act ending has an additional task, that of presenting a satisfactory conclusion to the action. There are several types of conclusions that work well for comedies. Three, in particular, have proven themselves very amenable for the type of comedies you will be creating. One is the ever-popular "Happy Ever After" conclusion. Boy gets girl, rides off into the sunset, et al. Your concluding laugh here will usually come from the protagonist himself (or herself), or from one of the protagonists, if there are more than one. The hero, for example could be saying something along the lines of how happy he is that they will now be able to get married.

```
He: I can't wait to hear you saying: "I
    promise to love, honor, and obey..."
She: Well, two out of three ain't bad.
     CURTAIN
```

The second type of conclusion is one that I am particularly fond of. It is the "Oh, No! Here We Go Again" scenario. I've used this successfully in several of my plays. Basically, it runs like this: just when everything is resolved nicely and everybody is ready to live happily ever after, something happens *just as the curtain is falling* to put the hero back into the soup again.

Now, this might sound like we have introduced another problem that is obviously not going to be resolved; but, it is a fulfilling conclusion from the audience's point of view because it leaves them convinced that the hero is one of those poor souls who is destined to spend his life in an endless cycle of getting into one predicament after the other.

An excellent example of this type of conclusion can be found in Kaufmann and Hart's classic comedy *The Man Who Came to Dinner*. In a nutshell, a pompous celebrity comes to have dinner at the hero's house, slips and falls, and is convalescing at the house. He causes all sorts of mischief from his sickbed, all the while threatening to sue him for a million dollars. At the conclusion, he has recovered and is finally convinced not to sue. As he is leaving the house, though, he again slips and falls, and as the curtain descends is screaming about how he now intends to sue for two million dollars.

In my play *Off With His Head*, the hero has gone through three acts of dealing with the spirits of kings and queens who are constantly threatening to have his head cut off. At the end, he has managed to send them all back to the netherworld and tells his wife:

```
HARRY: I just want to relax.  I don't
       want to hear about kings,queens,
       sorcerers or Grand High Priestesses.
       And one thing is for sure—I never
       want to hear anyone shout:
       "Off with his head!" again.
       (The front door bursts open and
       MARTHA, his mother-in-law, ENTERS,
       charging in.)
MARTHA: Harold Preston, you're trying to
       drive us all crazy!
       (She points her finger at HARRY
       and shouts:)
       I'll have your head for that!
       (HARRY groans, as...)
       THE CURTAIN FALLS
```

The third is a variety of the "Here We Go Again" ending. It's what I call the "Ironic Twist." The idea here is that the hero's problem has been resolved, but just before the final curtain, an identical problem unexpectedly arises for another principal. For this to work effectively, two things are necessary: First, that principal must be someone who has been instrumental in helping to resolve the hero's problem, and second, the *reason* he has been able to do so is that no one could possibly suspect that he would be susceptible to falling into the same predicament.

A very simplified example of this would be a situation where a teenager has started the chain of events that results in the primary problem of the play by employing some sort of falsehood. He or she could have lied about something, or perhaps turned in a school report about some daring exploit of a family member that never actually happened, and the ramifications of this action snowballs into a major dilemma for him or her. With the help of a kindly relative (uncle, aunt, grandfather, etc.), everything works out just fine. Just before the final curtain, that relative is delivering what would seem to be a concluding speech, something on the order of: "Now, you see what a tangled web we weave, etc., etc..." Just as he is doing so, the front door opens and IRS agents are on the doorstep demanding to know why he has listed his two dogs as dependent children on his income tax for the last ten years. This, of course, is followed by a quick fall of the curtain before he can respond verbally, but not before the audience has a chance to see his facial and bodily reaction.

The above types of endings are by no means the only way to conclude a amateur comedy. A close examination, however, of many of the notable and most memorable comedies that have been written for both professional and amateur stages will reveal that a great many have employed some variety of the three to ring down their third act curtains. It is a hackneyed cliche, but nothing really does succeed like success.

Chapter Six

The One Indispensable Tool

Before you begin the actual writing of plays that you intend to sell to the amateur market, a few words should be said about an indispensable tool of the playwright's craft: a personal computer. I know, I know, William Shakespeare got along just fine without a computer. This is true, but then again, the Bard's publishers, unlike those you will be dealing with, did not require him to submit soft copies of his manuscripts on disk in ASCII format.

Accept this as fact: you absolutely must use a computer to create the final draft of your scripts (what you will actually be sending to prospective publishers). There is no other way to approach the business, unless you are willing to endure the endless drudgery of typing draft after X-ed out, scribbled over draft. In addition, your publisher will charge you a hefty keying-in fee if you are not able to supply a soft copy (a copy on a computer disk) of your manuscript.

If your complaint is that you are not computer-literate, my answer is simple: *get* computer-literate. It's not that difficult, by the way. You do not have to become a "computer nerd" to understand the *basic* information you need to know in order to use a computer to create your plays. Moreover, a great number of books are available to help you. A good start would be

DOS For Dummies, or if you intend to purchase a new computer, *Windows 95 For Dummies.* The subtitle of books in this series: *A Guide For The Rest Of Us* says it all. This book and others in that genre are strictly for laymen—folks like you and me to whom a computer is a *tool* to accomplish specific tasks, rather than a hobby (or avocation!). They are written in clear English, rather than in techno-babble. A person of average intelligence can utilize them to understand what they need to know about using a computer to compose plays as easily as they can use a cookbook to learn how to bake a cake. The very fact that you are a writer indicates to me that you have a leg up Joe Six-Pack in the allocation of graymatter, so when I say that using a computer to write your plays will be a snap for you, I know I'm on safe ground.

Hardware

Here's the good news: You do not need to buy the latest and greatest equipment available. You may even be able to pick up what you need secondhand at the various computer shows that are proliferating. A great many of the bells and whistles currently pre-packaged in the computers you see advertised for two or three thousand dollars are not at all necessary for your needs. Here's what I suggest you get:

A computer with a 486DX2-66 processor. These are currently available secondhand and are quite reasonably priced. Computer stores push machines using even more advanced processors operating at speeds in excess of 100 MHz on people, whether or not (mostly not) they actually need the extra speed and processing power. The 66 MHz operating speed is more than fast enough to handle the word-processing applications you will need to use.

A SVGA color monitor. Try to get a slightly smaller screen size than dealers will try to sell you. A 14" monitor is fine. Above that size, the prices rise dramatically.

A 3 1/2" floppy disk drive. You probably don't have to ask for this. All computers of the 486 generation and higher have a 3 1/2" floppy drive as standard equipment. If you run into the oddball that has only a 5 1/4" drive (one with both sizes is fine) at a used computer show, pass it up. The 5 1/4" format is simply not used anymore.

A Laser-jet or Ink-jet printer. As with the computer itself, try to get a used printer that is a bit older. You'll save tons of money. Don't go for a color printer, by the way. You don't need it. In fact, if you submit a hard-copy script in anything but black ink on white paper, the odds are very strong that it will not get read. Dot matrix printers are cheaper, but they take forever to print up your manuscript, and if they are the older type that do not produce near-letter quality type, they will not create a copy that is easy enough for your publisher to read comfortably. Again—instant rejection.

A hard drive with at least 500 Megabytes of storage space if you are buying an older machine. A larger drive is not necessary unless you plan to purchase a new machine with a Windows 95 operating system and the latest programs installed. These newer programs require much more hard disk space than do older software. On a new machine, go for at least 1.5 Gigabytes.

At least 8 Megabytes of RAM. If your machine has 16 Megabytes or more, that is fine but the more RAM, the higher the price. You cannot operate efficiently, however, with less than 8 Megabytes. New machines routinely come with 16 or more Megabytes.

A mouse or track ball. Such a device is handy in DOS applications for moving around your document quickly and accessing pull-down menus, and is required for using Windows applications comfortably.

A FAX modem is not absolutely essential but is quite useful. Many publishers have Internet E-mail addresses, and this is a very fast way to get revisions, etc. of your script into their hands. Get one that operates at a baud rate of at least 14.4K. Higher baud rates process incoming and outgoing data faster, but will cost you more. Slower modems are a bother, and it is virtually impossible to comfortably access Internet Web pages with them. Some publishers have Web pages as well as E-mail addresses, and these pages have a listing of their writer's guidelines on them. Before too long, I suspect that most publishers will have Web pages. A FAX modem will also allow you to send FAX copies of your work right from your screen, a very useful function.

Another useful but not essential accessory is **a CD ROM drive.** This will allow you to use quick-reference tools such as encyclopedias, dictionaries, etc. that are published in CD-ROM format. A 4X drive is sufficient for your needs here. Faster drives will cost more, and for the text-based applications you will be using they are not really necessary.

You do *not* need a sound card and the external speakers that come with it. Sound cards are essentially used for games, and you do not want to be using your computer for games. It is too tempting to play a few hours of a popular game instead of producing your daily output of words.

Software

If you already computer literate, you may be comfortable working in DOS. The only drawback to working strictly in DOS is that you have to remember several multi-stroke commands. If not, you will want to work in a GUI (Graphic User Interface) environment such as Windows 95, where mouse clicks easily replace keystrokes. Word processing programs are readily available in either environment. Whichever word processor you select, make sure it has the following features:

- It must be capable of keeping at least six documents open at the same time.
- It must be capable of writing a soft copy of the files onto a floppy disk in the ASCII format.

Though it is not absolutely necessary, you might want to purchase low-end CAD (Computer Aided Drafting) software to create your stage diagrams. I use a program I paid under $100 for. Ask at a software store about an inexpensive CAD program that is easy to use.

Incidentally, if you buy a used machine, and copies of copyrighted programs are already loaded onto its hard drive, you will still need to purchase copies of any software you choose to use and register them. You can erase the ones you don't want to use. That is the only legal way to use software. Using software without paying for the privilege is illegal. Since you wouldn't want anyone to perform your plays without payment of a royalty, don't use copyrighted software unless you legally own your copy.

Incidentally, I do not wish to imply that you *have* to buy an older machine, only that it is much cheaper if you do, and a 486-based machine will do everything you need it to do as a playwright. If you have the money and want to buy a newer machine directly from a computer retailer, please don't let me dissuade you. Be sure the programs you buy, though, are compatible with the processor of whichever machine you decide upon.

Chapter Seven

"At Rise"

Once you have come up with a basic idea for your play, created the characters who will bring it to life on the stage, and devised the framework of the plot that they will work within, you are ready to begin the actual writing of your script. After you have typed the magic words "Act One" at the top of your first page, the first thing to do is to describe the setting of the play.

Your verbal depiction of the set at the start of the first act will go under the heading: "Setting" (surprise, surprise). See the chapter on Manuscript Preparation for the proper way to format this information on the printed manuscript page.

Begin the description of your set with a statement that immediately tells us where we are, but yet remains broad, such as: *The living room of George and Ann Driscoll's apartment in a Manhattan high-rise* or *A deluxe suite at the Grand Plaza Hotel* or *The family room of the Prestons' home in Santa Fe.* For an outdoor set, you might begin with a statement such as: *A park bench in a wooded area of Central Park* or *A grassy area under the shade of a large elm tree.*

You don't have to specify the city (or even the state or country) if you don't want to unless it is important to the plot. If you want to set your play in a small town, but it does not matter exactly where that town is, you can indicate this in that first statement. One of the opening sentences above could just as easily read: *The family room of the Prestons' home in a rural town somewhere in the American Southwest.* You could even leave out the "somewhere in the American Southwest" part, if that is not needed. Recall that the more flexible you make your play, the broader its appeal will be.

This is followed by any specific information the reader (and the set designer) needs to know about the general ambiance of the set: *The room and its furnishings have a look of faded glory. At one time, they may have been sparkling and in the height of fashion, but now appear to be worn and in need of replacement.* Or perhaps a set that is the complete opposite: *There is a feel of vitality and energy about the room. The colors are bright and sparkle with the exuberance of youth.*

Next, locate and describe all means of entrance to and egress from the set: *A doorway along the left wall below center leads to the kitchen (offstage). A short, three-step stairway in the extreme upstage right corner leads to a door that opens to the bedrooms (offstage). A set of french doors along the upstage wall, left of center opens to a patio.*

Finally, give a brief rundown on the pieces of on-stage furniture and their placement: *There is a furniture grouping consisting of sofa, armchair, and small end table downstage, left of center. Along the upstage wall can be found a large bookcase filled with knick-knacks, piles of magazines, an assorted stack of LPs, and a few empty soda cans (in short, everything but books!). A small table Up Right holds a vintage 1960s rotary phone. There is a small chair alongside this table, just below it.*

As has been mentioned before, try not to be too restrictive in your choice of furniture. Amateur groups need to be able to pick up their stage furnishings and decorations primarily from secondhand stores, donations from cast members' families, and a careful scouting out of the neighborhood on bulk trash collection days. Unless you absolutely have to; i. e., it is *indispensable* to the plot, try not to call for specific pieces that cannot be substituted for (a distinctive type of dining table or style of chair, for example).

You will be providing a set diagram that provides

much of this information, but it is still necessary to *briefly* describe your set in the manner indicated above at the beginning of Act One.

I have found it very helpful to tape or staple a sketch of my set diagram to a piece of corrugated cardboard, and using colored push-pins to represent the various characters, keep an ongoing record of who is on-stage at any given moment as I am writing the play. I strongly recommend you do likewise for several reasons. For openers, it will keep you from flipping back through pages of dialog to find out if you have had a character you now need to speak exit earlier. In addition, knowing who is on-stage will help you to shape the dialog. A line directed to a single character is likely to be phrased differently if it is spoken to a group of characters.

There are four basic ways to have the action of a play begin.

Here's another reason: as important as it is to know who is on-stage, it is even of more consequence to you, the playwright, to know who is *not*. If, for example, a teenage character is telling her friend how she plans to sneak out tonight to go to a rock concert, it would be quite embarrassing to find out that you have forgotten to have her parents exit before she blurts this information out.

Last, but certainly far from least, keeping an accurate record of who is where will help you to avoid having a character on-stage doing and saying nothing for long periods of time (something you should never do!).

Now, you are ready to begin the action—almost. You need to describe *exactly* what is going on on-stage as the curtain goes up. This is accomplished by use of the phrase "At Rise." The Act Curtains (the main curtains that separate the audience from the stage) of almost all professional theaters "rise" or move straight up. It is likely that the audiences for your plays will have the opening scene revealed to them via

Act Curtains that are drawn from the middle to either side, rather than rising. Most high school auditoriums do not have enough fly space (room above the top of the proscenium) to have their curtains rise. Nevertheless, the playwriting convention that describes the opening of a play is known as "At Rise." Using any other words will flag you as a non-professional at this business, an impression you definitely do not want a potential publisher to get.

There are four basic ways to have the action of a play begin: *An Unpopulated opening, a Discovery opening, a Stage-in-Motion opening and a Freeze-Frame opening.*

An Unpopulated opening is exactly what you might expect it to be. No actors are on-stage, and none enter until the curtain is fully up. This is particularly effective if there is some aspect of the set that you want the audience to pick up immediately, such as crossed battle-axes over the fireplace mantle, or a exceptionally stunning (or exceptionally grotesque) portrait on a wall. The audience's attention will be directed toward this prominent feature of your set without the distraction of an actor moving about.

Be forewarned, though. If you intentionally draw your audience's attention to a certain item on-stage, you had better make sure that that object plays an important role in your plot. There is nothing more frustrating to an audience than sitting through three acts of a play waiting for you to bring an object into the action, only to see the final curtain fall without that happening.

> You need to describe exactly what is going on on-stage as the curtain goes up.

Directed attention to a set feature is not the only purpose of an Unpopulated opening, of course. Sometimes a playwright simply wishes to have his characters make an entrance onto the stage rather than having one or more of them on-stage at curtain rise.

With a Discovery-type opening, an actor or several actors are on-stage as the curtain rises; however, they are either seated or are standing immobile, and so are "discovered" by the audience shortly after they take in the set.

Unpopulated and Discovery openings are the easiest to manage for a director of an amateur show, who will be working primarily with inexperienced actors. You should give this strong consideration when writing an amateur play.

The remaining two types of openings are a bit trickier and work best when carried out by actors with more experience. A Stage-in-Motion opening is exactly what it sounds like it might be. The curtain rises to a stage where one or more of the actors on-stage are moving from one place to another. To be most effective, this must be well-timed and requires coordination between the stage manager, curtain puller, and the actors who will be in motion. Actors must know *exactly* when to begin their move, so as to be where the director wants them to be when they are revealed by the rising curtain. If they start to move too soon they be forced to stop short before the curtain is fully up. Too late, and they will have to take larger strides. Either way, they will be out of position or arriving at their position awkwardly. That's why I suggest leaving this opening to plays written for the professional or semi-professional stage.

> Unpopulated and Discovery openings are the easiest to manage.

Freeze-Frame involves having a stage filled with actors who are "caught" snapshotlike, frozen in the middle of some sort of movement or action. A beat or two after the curtain is fully up, they simultaneously begin to move, as if a switch has been moved from "off" to "on." This technique is most often employed by directors of musicals that open with a chorus number or to movement synchronized to music. I use it myself whenever I direct a production of *My Fair Lady*, which opens to a scene in front of the Covent Garden Opera

House. Buskers go into their act and flower girls roam through the crowd of people leaving the opera in orchestrated movements backed by music.

Freeze-Frame is generally not called for in the script, but remains a director's option to the Stage-in-Motion type of opening that would be the only other alternative in such a situation. As with the Stage-in-Motion opening, it is a tricky maneuver to carry out, hence you should never specify that it be used to begin a play written for amateur use.

Regardless of the type of opening you decide to use, you need to begin your description of what is going on on-stage "At Rise" with the time of day and, *if relevant*, the time of year (the season, the month, the day of the week, etc.). Don't bore the readers of your script by telling them that the play opens on "the second Tuesday in June," unless that is pertinent to the plot. If your play needs to begin on a special day (Christmas, Thanksgiving, etc.), state that.

Typical "At Rise" information might begin: *It is early evening* or *It is a summer morning*. It might, of course, be necessary to be much more specific Let's say your plot concerns some hijinks that revolve around the filing of income tax returns. Your "At Rise" particulars might start something like this: *It is April 8, one week before the dreaded tax filing deadline.*

You will now proceed to give an explanation of what is going on on-stage when the play begins as explained above. Be brief. You're not writing a novel. A play is an audio-visual medium, and between the Setting information and the dialog, your readers will be able to figure out everything they need to know without too much verbal blandishment.

With that accomplished, the next thing you need to do...is pause. Before you begin writing the dialog, you should spend some time "walking" the characters who are on-stage at curtain rise or shortly thereafter through their first few lines in your mind. More about this in the next chapter.

Chapter Eight

Dialog—Act One

Throughout the chapters on dialog, there is one thing that you must keep in mind. (I'll help you to keep it in mind because I will *continually* be harping on the point.) It is this: Don't ever just sit and write dialog. Always run the portion of the scene you are about to commit to paper through your head first.

Even at the very start of your play, you should be acquainted with your characters. You have created a personality, a "life" if you will, for them on your character sheets. Because of this, you should be able to envision them saying your lines. "See" them moving about the stage and speaking the dialog. Is there anything about the lines you are planning to assign to them that goes counter to their personality—something that doesn't ring true when they say those lines? If you're not happy with what you "hear," "rewind the tape" and run it over again with new lines until you are. Then capture that dialog and write it down quickly.

I attribute much of my own success as a playwright to working in this manner. There is a *big* difference between what looks good on paper and what plays well onstage. Envisioning your characters walking through each portion of your play and speaking the lines before you commit each segment of dialog to paper is a way of bridging that gap. It will give you a simulation of what your play will actually look and sound like on-stage when real, live actors will have to convince an audience to believe in the characters you have created.

Once you have jotted down the results of your little private performance by your characters, you will have a rough draft of the dialog for the sequence you are working on. These lines will still need some work before you are ready to include them in the scene; however, you now have the gist of what is to be said for this portion of the scene, and which of your characters will be saying it. Subsequent chapters of this book will deal with precisely what must be done to polish your lines for stage presentation. The sequence of the speeches, the word order within individual lines, the trimming of unneeded words, etc. are some of the finishing touches that we will work on later.

At this point, you have a decision to make. Allow me to say at the outset that the two choices I am about to present to you are equally valid methods of approaching the business of dialog creation. Feel free to use whichever you are the most comfortable with.

Choice #1: Move through your play bit by bit, as explained above, without pausing to do any further work on the dialog for now. Continue working like this right up until the moment the curtain descends on Act Three. Then go back to the opening of Act One and begin to work on the individual speeches (there will be a lot to do!) until you have an entire polished script.

The advantages of this method are that you will have a virtually intact plot when you finish the rough draft, and you no longer have to figure out "what comes next." In addition, there will be fewer inconsistencies, as Acts One and Two will still be fresh in your mind while you are working on Act Three. The shorter the time between writing the dialog for the opening first act scene and that which brings down the final curtain, the less likely you are to have a character who is twenty-three years old and has two sisters and a brother in Act One, and is twenty-one years old with two brothers and a sister in Act Three. (Of course, if you religiously keep your character sheets up to date as you work *and refer to them often*, you won't have this problem at all!)

The major disadvantage is that the individual bits you will be working on one by one after the rough draft is completed will *not* be as fresh in your mind as they would have been had you paused to work on them before moving on. Your little mental run-throughs will have been forgotten, and all you are left with of them is whatever you have written down. If a particular section needs *content* revision (as opposed to dialog revision) because an inconsistency has developed in a subsequent portion of the play, you may be forced to begin the process of running it through your head all over again to get things straight.

Another disadvantage is that while your finished play will undoubtedly be closer to that envisioned in your plot framework, you may lose opportunities to have it grow in alternate (and perhaps better) directions as you race through to the finish line with the draft.

Choice #2: Do not leave this portion of the scene until everything about the dialog for it is just right and is polished using the guidelines that will be explained in later chapters. Proceed, slowly and methodically, scene fragment by scene fragment, until you reach the final curtain (then stop!).

The advantages of working in this manner are that when you are finished, you are finished. Except for the inevitable spit-and-polish that will be applied here and there, when you type CURTAIN at the end of the third act, your manuscript will soon be on its way to the first publisher on your list.

In addition, every sequence is fresh in your mind as you work on it. This will present more possibilities for the inclusion of additional jokes and funny bits in your script.

The disadvantages are mainly psychological. There is a tendency to be somewhat discouraged if after a month or two of work on your dialog, you still haven't gotten beyond the first act. You can counter this by pausing now and then to read what you have already created. There is nothing quite as uplifting to a playwright as reading through a dozen or so pages and being able to say to himself or herself: "Hey, that's good!"

You're going to ask anyway, so I guess I'll tell you now and get it over with. Except for short-shorts (one-act plays that consist of about ten to twelve minutes of playing time), I always rely on "Choice #2." I like to leave things all neat and tidy behind me as I proceed. I know this could probably be classified as an indication of "retentive" behavior characteristics, but Freud-be-damned, that's the way I am comfortable writing. It works for me, and I make money writing plays in this manner. As I've already mentioned, though, you can succeed as a playwright very nicely using either method, so take Frank Sinatra's (and Burger King's) advice, and do it your way.

Identifying Your Characters

Once you have the curtain up and you have some of your characters on-stage and ready to speak, you need to let your audience know who they are. Since this is not a businessman's convention, where everybody walks around with little tags that say: "Hello, My name is..." pasted on their jackets, you will have to identify them through your dialog.

Smoothly identifying the characters via dialog is part of the task of exposition.

This is really quite simple. The easiest way is to merely have the characters address each other by name or relationship (Mom, Dad, etc.) during their first few lines. The trick, though, is doing so in a manner that does not hang a big flag out that announces to the audience: "Attention: I am now identifying my characters!"

There is an effective way to accomplish the naming process seamlessly. Start by having the first or second line directed to someone start or end with that person's name or relationship:

> *Bill, where are you going?*
> *Are you looking for something, Gail?*
> *I'm down here, Mom.*

As an alternative, you can always have the name appear in the middle of a line, as it sometimes does in the course of normal conversation:

> *As I told you before, Alice, I just don't have the*
> *time to go shopping with you during finals week.*

The person addressed should respond with a line that similarly identifies the first speaker. Follow with a few lines (no more than two each) that does not have the name embedded within them, then hit your audience with one more set of lines that does. At this point, the task of naming these characters is over. The names have been mentioned twice in the span of six or eight lines of dialog. Who's who should now be clear in your audience's mind. There is no further need to have the lines appended with mention of the characters' monikers, so don't! Continual repetition of character names within the dialog will quickly bore the audience.

As new people enter the scene, use a similar approach to identifying them; i.e., mention their names in the first line directed to each, wait a line or two, and then repeat it once more. The only difference is that there is no need for the newcomers to use the names of those already known to the audience in their replies.

There are exceptions. Sometimes it would be unnatural for someone who enters not to use a name in replying. For instance, a doctor or repairman who arrives at the front door would not just say: "Hi." A skilled playwright can use this to his or her advantage, however. A character who has been called only Mom, Dad, Uncle Joe, etc. to this point can have themselves further identified by the entering actor with a line such a as:

> *Good afternoon, Mrs. Johnson.*

Smoothly identifying the characters via dialog is part of the task of *exposition*, one of the two functions of dialog in all dramatic presentations. The other is *plot development*. In comedies, dialog is used for the additional purpose of injecting *humor*. Sets of lines can be inserted in comedies strictly for a good (it is hoped!) laugh, without any other "redeeming social merit." Let's take a closer look at the mechanics of these three operations.

Exposition

Of necessity, much of the play's exposition will be interlaced with plot development during the dialog of Act One. As I mentioned, you have already begun the task of exposition in the naming of your characters. There are a few things to remember about your first act exposition. First off, don't try to hit the audience with too much within a short period of time. I know that you'd like to get all that messy exposition out of the way right away, and move on to writing some snappy dialog that will leave 'em rolling in the aisles. Don't succumb to the temptation. If you do, three things will happen: (a) You will be hanging out another flag, one that declares: "Attention, the following dialog is exposition." (b) You will bore your audience to tears. (c) They will forget most of it, anyway!

A good rule of thumb is to tell them only what they *need* to know at any point. As the play progresses and it becomes necessary for them to know something else, tell it to them then. Take the instance of our old Uncle Charley, who left behind the treasure chest with the stolen statuette of an ancient god in it. If you were actually writing this play, some expository information about Uncle Charley would have to come out in the dialog when the chest is first introduced to the audience. They would probably have to know that he was an Indiana-Jones-type, who spent his life on fortune hunting quests. What they *wouldn't* have to be told at the outset is that he was hunting for treasure in old Incan or Aztec ruins (where he came across the statuette). People inevitably associate such ruins with sacred idols. If they were told ahead of time that Uncle Charley was poking around in such places, the significance of the statuette would be "telegraphed" to the audience. As soon as it was retrieved from the chest, they would instinctively know (or strongly suspect) that the plot was going to revolve around it. Uncle Charley barging in, in search of it, and the breaking of the statuette just as he did would become anticlimactic events. Your plot would have become *predictable*, a circumstance you don't ever want to occur.

Another problem with attempts at dumping carloads of exposition all at once is that the resultant dialog inevitably becomes "novelized." That is, all sorts of information that is essentially useless within the framework of the play will start spewing from the characters' mouths. The dialog printed in a novel is usually *much* more elaborate than stage dialog. Dialog is one of the principal tools a novelist has to bring out the personality of his or her characters. You are going to have real, live actors to do this. Recall that a successful performance is a collaboration between playwright, director, and actors. Let the actors do their part!

Try to make your exposition as transparent as you can. The trick is to make each bit of information that you are feeding to the audience seem like an incidental part of the lines being spoken. This can be done with dialog that is primarily plot development or even with speeches that are essentially incidental humor.

An illustration is in order here. Three pages into the dialog of Act One of a new play I am currently working on, I needed to let the audience know that the protagonist's aunt, with whom she lives, runs a boarding house. In addition, I wanted to clearly identify the group of people who are about to enter en masse as her boarders, rather than relatives. I was able to accomplish all of this in the course of a four line joke:

```
    AURORA: That will have to wait.  It's time for
            dinner. I'm about to ring the bell.
            (She moves to the table and picks
            up the hand bell.)
  SAMANTHA: Oh no! The charge of the Boarder Patrol!
      GAIL: Border Patrol? We're 100 miles
            from the border.
  SAMANTHA: Not the United States borders—my
```

```
aunt's boarders! Take cover, Gail!
(She pushes GAIL into the alcove
between the stairs and the bookcase
as AURORA rings the hand bell. Within
seconds, several of the boarders begin
pouring both down the stairs and
through the front doorway. All are
in a headlong rush to get to
the dinner table.)
```

At the conclusion of this dialog, six characters make their first entrance. The audience knows without question that each is a boarder in a boarding house run by Aurora (Samantha's aunt). All of this was accomplished without the flag of exposition being waved. I got a laugh out of it, too!

In the ensuing dialog between the boarders as they grab for the food, I manage to quickly have all of them identified by name and also establish the fact that three are normals and three are eccentrics. When the play is published, as I am certain it will be (humility is not a very useful virtue to a playwright!), you can buy a copy and see how[1].

One final point needs to be made about your Act One exposition. Don't feel obliged to introduce all of your principal characters in the first act. If a character isn't needed until the second or third act, introduce him or her *then*. Bringing principals in for no other reason than having the audience get a look at them (and getting the exposition of those characters over with!) will undoubtedly prove to be counterproductive. Audiences have short memories. If they haven't completely forgotten who the characters are already, they'll spend mental time trying to remember (all the way back to Act One!).

Either way, your play will suffer. In the first case, the condition where they are essentially clueless as to who the characters are, they will be expecting you to tell them with

---

1.If you are interested, drop me an e-mail (my addresses are given at the back of the book). Once it has been published, I will let you know from which publisher it can be purchased as well as the title. (I never divulge the title of a work in progress until it is sold - a personal superstition.)

some expository dialog. Since you've felt that you have already done so back in Act One, you won't waste lines doing it again. They will either stare with blank faces as important dialog goes by them or turn to a companion to say: "Who *is* that? Do you know?" Now, even if the companion has a Mensa-level IQ, and actually has remembered the characters from their original appearances, that person will *also* miss important dialog as he or she fills the other in. If, on the other hand, people do vaguely recall seeing the characters, they will *still* miss out on some of the action as their mental RAM stops accepting input from the stage while it desperately try to access the cranial directories and sub-directories where information about those characters has been stored.

> Picture the characters on your set, drop the problem in their laps, and see what develops.

The exception (there are *always* exceptions!) is when you are introducing a character at the very end of Act One for your curtain-falling twist, as explained in Chapter Five. Since he or she will be used again immediately when the next act commences, you can trust your audience to retain knowledge of them during the intermission.

Plot Development

Now that you understand how to work the required exposition into your dialog, let's superimpose your plot onto Act One. Remember that this will be a plot *framework*, guidelines to provide structure to the action. Don't let it become a strict template, from which no deviation is allowed. Without structure your play will just meander around for two hours and never get anywhere. If the structure is too rigid, though, it will still get somewhere, but you and your audience will probably not be pleased about how it got there. Be flexible!

The only thing that absolutely has to happen in this act is the introduction of the problem (or at least the first of the "problems" if there are more than one) that the protagonist is going to have to deal with. The sooner you do this, the better. Once the audience knows who is who and any other bits of information that they have to have knowledge of for the problem to be understood, it is time to get your protagonist (or protagonists) up that tree via the dialog.

What we are going to do is throw the situation at the characters and see how they handle it. Start by trying to envision the totality of the problem's introduction in your head. Then "see" your characters bringing out the problem through their speeches. This is a somewhat larger task than the smaller portions of the scene that I want you to run through your mind before writing down the dialog for them. I don't expect you to remember and immediately write down picture-perfect dialog for such a big chunk of the action. In fact, unless some brilliant speeches pop into your head (you'll want write those down immediately before you forget them), it is fine to just sketch out the sequence of events, once you and your characters agree on what they will be.

A personal note: I like to devote quite a bit of time to this, as it is critical to the success of the play. I usually put some soothing music on the stereo, and settle back in an easy chair with a yellow[2] lined pad and pencil on my lap. (I don't use the computer here because I am not actually going to create dialog; I am just going to set down events. I need to be relaxed to concentrate, and I can't do that with my laptop balanced on my large, economy-sized belly.)

Picture the characters on your set, drop the problem in their laps, and see what develops.

Inevitably, you will have to run it by them several times and introduce it to them in several different ways. If it does not seem to be going anywhere after several run-throughs, try a permutation of the problem (a change in the

2. The pad is a yellow legal-sized pad in deference to Moss Hart, one of my idols as a playwright. If you haven't yet read his brilliant and inspiring autobiography, *Act One*, do yourself a favor and do so. Then you'll understand both my use of a yellow legal pad and why he is one of my idols.

nature or perhaps the gravity of the problem) on them. If that still doesn't work, and you have planned to have more than one problem, put the first aside and work on the second. If that results in the generation of a satisfactory and workable chain of events, take the time to turn it into dialog using the method described earlier.

This, of course, still leaves you with the need to work the original problem into the play. Sometimes, you'll find that the circumstances and subsequent dialog that went into the creation of the second have given you a natural lead-in to introduction of the first. (You will be surprised at how often this happens!) Even if it doesn't, you are not all the way back to square one. You still have several pages of dialog "in the bank." Of greater importance, in the process of writing them, you have become more familiar with your characters. By now, natural speech patterns for each character introduced will have been established, and you will have learned more about what makes each of them tick. Now you have more to work with, and that may just be the edge you need to successfully introduce the first problem.

Don't try to "save" the play's humor for Acts Two and Three.

There are times when you'll realize that you no longer need that first problem, so you can drop it. This will, of necessity, cause revisions to your original plot outline to accommodate this, but as has been said often enough in this book, that is why flexibility is the key to successful playwriting.

Adding The Humor

Always keep in mind as you write dialog that you are writing a comedy, and a comedy needs laughs. If you've done your homework, that is, generated detailed character sheets for each principal and assigned sufficiently funny traits to each eccentric as well as to each normal who you would like to deliver some funny lines, the humor should flow naturally from your characters as they speak and react to what is going on on-stage. Opportunities to add a joke or funny situation should continually present themselves during your little mental run-throughs for both exposition and plot development dialog. Use them! Never hesitate to insert the laugh lines and situations that occur to you at any point in the play because you think you need to be doing something else with your dialog just then.

Every audience is different.

Executed properly, the jokes will become a *part* of your exposition or plot development. Don't explain an eccentric trait of your character, *show it via one or more jokes.* Find a way to humorously introduce your problems. Find an even funnier way to resolve them.

Be aware that you can write your entire play, using all the required elements for its construction, by moving *directly* from one joke to the next. It takes practice to do this well, but it is the hallmark of skillfully crafted comedy.

Don't try to "save" the play's humor for Acts Two and Three. If you don't make your audience laugh heartily and often in the first act, you've lost them. Even if your remaining two acts are loaded with surefire rib ticklers, your jokes will fall flat. You have to get your audience "used to" laughing at the dialog and the things that are happening.

An audience is a strange animal. (Some are stranger than others.) You might go through a hundred performances where certain lines never fail to have them rolling in the aisles. Then, for no apparent reason, the audience for the 101st will sit quietly through your best gag lines, but will laugh hysterically at something that isn't even funny! Further, *every* audience is different. Some will begin laughing immediately and never let up until the final curtain. Others take forever to warm up. Some never do!

Your job as the playwright of an amateur comedy is to

do everything in your power to start them laughing early. Once the ice has been broken and a good laugh is experienced by all, the natural reluctance of each individual attendee to laugh out loud without fear of someone looking at them strangely has been overcome. They will then feel free to titter, snicker, chuckle, and guffaw their way through the rest of the play. Keep them laughing through the first act, and you will own them for the remaining two!

I have not, incidentally, included separate chapters that deal with dialog specifically written for Acts Two and Three. The chapters on plotting, the mechanics of dialog, and on writing comedy for the stage cover everything you will need to know to successfully script the final two acts.

Chapter Nine

The Mechanics Of Dialog

Types Of Dialog

Stage dialog bears little resemblance to that written for a novel. If you have read several works for the stage[1], you might have noticed the difference (even if, at this point, you're not quite sure what that difference is). What you probably *don't* know is that it also differs greatly from the everyday conversations people have at their homes, offices, or on the street.

Let's take a closer look at each type of dialog so we can see why. Novel dialog is generally the most descriptive of the three. The primary reason for this is that the written word is the only tool available to a novelist. It must be used to paint a vivid picture of every locale in the story, provide the ambiance, and push the plot along. In addition, the novel writer

---

1. If you *haven't* already read several plays, what are you waiting for? You can't expect to create effective material for the stage without spending a great deal of time *reading* the scripts of plays. Make a study of the works of playwrights you admire, particularly those who have excelled at writing comedies. Also, purchase scripts to the most popular amateur plays from the publishers listed in the chapter on "Markets," and try to figure out *why* they have been so successful. (If you're not sure which plays in any given amateur catalog have been produced most frequently, ask the publisher. He or she will be happy to tell you.)

must describe exactly what each character looks like, what that character's traits are, what motivates him or her to do whatever they do, etc. Instead of expending page upon page of descriptive prose to do all this (very boring), the experienced novelist will build much of it into the dialog.

This detailed approach to dialog is not needed onstage, since theater is a visual medium. People can *see* what the sets and characters look like, so they don't have to be told. There is no need for the players on-stage to speak lines filled with flowery adjectives to describe things that can be plainly seen by all in attendance.

Stage dialog is characterized by a notable lack of descriptives. Besides being unnecessary, they could also become a serious detriment to the ability of your actors to give effective performances. The denizens of the worlds of prose fiction, you see, have a big advantage over the actors who will have to say your lines. They don't have to pause in the middle of a long sentence to breathe! Every line you write has to be spoken out loud by living, *breathing* actors. If you load your speeches with unneeded words, the actors will have to pause in the middle of them to take in a lungful of air. This will, without a doubt, disturb the rhythm of any actor, resulting in an uneven and wooden performance.

As any acting coach will tell you, an actor cannot begin to *act* until he or she has committed the lines to memory, and can rattle them off without any conscious effort. Only then, can the actor concentrate all of his effort on characterization so that he can give an effective and believable performance. If an actor has to speak sentences that are so long that he will have to pause somewhere to take a breath, he will have to devote attention to *where* he breaks the line each time he has to say it. In doing so, he runs the risk of falling out of character at that point, and a noticeable flat spot in his performance will occur every time.

As the writer of dialog for an amateur play, you have the *additional* challenge of writing lines that are not only capable of being said in a single breath, but are also *easy to learn*. The actors who have to work with your dialog will not be professionals. Your speeches should flow naturally; that is, one line should provide a logical cue for the next. They should not be constructed in such a manner that actors will "get lost" during performances, when they will not have a prompt book in their hands. This can happen very easily if the cues don't logically follow one another.

In addition, you should avoid long monologues. While they may be the staple of Shakespearian dramatic fare, and work very effectively in plays by O'Neill, Albee or Stoppard,[2] their effectiveness depends on the ability of talented actors to put them across competently and convincingly. When attempted by the performers of high school plays, they will fall flat every time. The young actors will be very uncomfortable as they try to work their way through monologues (or even remember all the words to them!), and it will show. Moreover,

Stage dialog is characterized by a notable lack of descriptives.

their discomfort will be nothing compared to the that of those who have to listen to them recite (for that is inevitably what they will do) long stretches of unbroken verbiage. The fidget rate of the audience will quickly go off the scale, and once again you will have lost them.

As a rule of thumb, I try not to let any character say more than three sentences without some sort of break. That break could come in the form of a responding character's line or some bit of business that forces the person to stop speaking to accomplish it (as opposed to business designed to occur as the lines are being spoken). An example of the type of business that could cause an actor to pause during a speech would be the task of answering the doorbell or a knock on the door.

Carrying on a conversation on the telephone would, of

2. If you are unfamiliar with any of these names, see footnote one!

course, have built-in pauses (while the unheard person on the other end of the line responds), so my three-line "rule" wouldn't apply here.

Long speeches also run the risk of becoming too "theatrical," when put into the hands of untrained actors. They provide opportunities for the type of overacting that could have the audience groaning and prove fatal to your play. Four or five lines into a monologue will find many amateur actors doing something like putting the back of their hand to their forehead to register dismay. Ugh!

You want to keep the actors speaking lines that will allow them to approach their roles naturally, without resorting to the employment of artificial claptrap. Which is not to say that you should have them speaking on-stage *exactly* they way they do on the street. This is an equally unacceptable use of dialog.

Recall that I said that there was as great a difference between stage dialog and everyday speech as there was between lines written for the stage and those found in novels. If you make a recording of the conversations that go on at home or at your place of business and then play it back, you will see why. People talk to each other in a herky-jerky, fragmented way. They will use sentences that aren't sentences. They will answer question with monosyllabic responses or with non-words (grunts, verbal shrugs, etc.).

> Each line written for the stage has a specific purpose in the script.

A typical exchange will go something like this:
"J'eat?"
"Nope. J'you?"
"Nah."
"Wanna gofer pizza?"
"Awright."

In short, what passes for acceptable everyday discourse would not be understood by many of the people in the audience, and would bore those who did. On stage, every line counts, and must contribute to either exposition, plot development, or humor (or a combination thereof) and must do so in a clear, intelligible manner.

The trick is to make your dialog sound as if it was normal conversation, while using the dramatist's artistry to create effective theatrical speeches for your characters. The difference is the same as that between a photograph and a painting. One is a exact image as seen by the lens with all the imperfections of the real life vista faithfully reproduced. The other is an *artistic* representation of the same scene. A painter uses all the tricks of his or her trade to emphasize particular aspects of a scene that are key to the representation of it on any given canvas. Likewise, he will use other "tricks" to de-emphasize things of lesser importance. Unimportant aspects will simply be eliminated. Two important tricks of *your* trade are *omission of unnecessary verbiage* and *word placement and order.*

Omission Of Unnecessary Verbiage

Each line written for the stage has a *specific* purpose in the script. If you have written a series of lines and you can't identify what their purpose is, you should re-examine that dialog to see if it can be eliminated. This verbal economy is one of the major differences between conversational speech and theatrical dialog.

Most of our day-to-day discourse has no real purpose, if we bother to look at it closely. Many times we speak to each other for no other reason that to flap our gums. We say: "How are you," to people we meet, when we really don't care or even want to know. There are times when we say some things that are really stupid just, it seems, to hear the sound of our own voices. A person will come in wearing a sopping raincoat and carrying a dripping umbrella, and someone else will invariably ask: "Is it raining?" (My standard answer to this, by the way, is: "No. Today I decided to get dressed and then take my shower, just for a change.") Or we say things like: "Hot enough for you?" or "So, you're another year older."

Lines such as these are without any meaningful purpose, and, hence, have no place on-stage. The only exception would be if you have them spoken by a character who you quickly want to establish as a total bore. In such a case, this trivial dialog would have *that* specific purpose, and would be acceptable. (Go easy with these kinds of lines, however, lest your *play* be judged a total bore!)

If you have determined that lines you have just written do have a purpose, they are "keepers"—almost. You still need to go over them to cull out any unnecessary words within those lines. Extraneous words bog down lines and may mask the intended purpose of the speech. Moreover, as has been explained above, they cause the actor to expend more breath on the line. Of equal importance, they force the performers to expend more of their *voice*. Remember that actors will be projecting their voices (it is hoped!) for the entire performance. They will be speaking above their normal volume for two hours each night. Since they are amateurs and have not had the vocal training that professionals have, they could end up hoarse by the end of the show.

One of the ways inexperienced playwrights have of using unnecessary words is by repeating things that have just been said:

> MOTHER: Billy, put your toys away.
> BILLY: My toys! But Mom, I *need* them.
> MOTHER: You need them? What you *need* is
> a good swat on your backside.
> And you'll get that if those toys
> aren't put away right now!

Now, let's get out our blue pencil and get rid of everything that is not needed in the last two lines:

> BILLY: But Mom, I *need* them.
> MOTHER: What you *need* is a good swat
> on your backside.

The thought has been communicated just as completely with less than half of the original words. And we still get a laugh out of them. Actually, the laugh is much more effective using the edited dialog for reasons that will be explained below. The economic use of words is another of the keys to successful playwriting.

Another way unnecessary verbiage works its way into scripts is by playwrights' attempts to *faithfully* reproduce the manner of speech they hear daily in the dialog that they write. When you run sequences through your head, you will inevitably "hear" your characters speaking in the speech patterns that you are most familiar with, i.e., those that are either your own or those of people you associate with daily. When you translate this into speeches for your play, you will have to edit out the superfluous bits that inevitably creep into everyday conversations.

It goes without saying (though I will say it anyway) that the little sputters and stammers that riddle our daily discourse are out. Unless your character really is *supposed to be* at a loss for words at a given point in the script, he should *not* be uttering things such as um, uh, er, and so forth. Likewise, interjections of such verbal effluvia as: "you know," "like," and "right" should never spew forth from your keyboard.

Among the words that should regularly be trimmed from your dialog are current "in" expressions. Search them out and eliminate same as vigorously as you might hunt down the weeds that choke the flowers and vegetables in your garden. In addition to being superfluous (as they inevitably are), they will *date* your play and severely limit the time span over which you expect to harvest the fruits of your labor (royalties!). Though you may think it makes your characters appear to be "with it," you'll be surprised how quickly they will become *without* it, as the expressions they use become *passe*.

On the subject of things that can date scripts, amateur plays should be free of references to people or events currently in the public eye. Many celebrities who are now experiencing their "fifteen minutes of fame" will quickly, quietly, and completely fade from the scene within a few years (sometimes, within a few months!). And nothing is as proverbially stale as yesterday's news. A fast way to lose an audience is to make them say to themselves: "Huh? What are they talking about? Did I miss something?"

If you feel the burning desire to refer to a news event or a celebrity within the lines of your play, make sure you choose one whose recognizability has been established beyond a doubt for a long period of time. The notoriety of the event or the fame of the celebrity should, at the very least, border on being legendary. The goal here is to guarantee that fifty years[3] from now your lines will not leave an audience scratching its collective head in bewilderment if a name is dropped or an event is referred to. You're probably safe with such names as Bogart, Sinatra, Abbott and Costello, The Three Stooges, etc. There's also no chance that events such as the Civil War, the Kennedy Assassination or the Moon Landings will ever be lost to historical obscurity, so you can get away with mentioning them. Better still, though—keep *all* the people and events in your script fictional and you'll never have to worry.

Another pitfall to avoid in order to keep your play from becoming dated is the use of prices. Inflation is an ongoing fact of life, and if you mention the price of a commonly available item (milk, gasoline, etc) in your script, audiences ten (or even five!) years in the future will be laughing about something you do not want them to laugh at when they hear the dialog! Directors could, of course, update the prices; however, doing so is technically in violation of the performance contract with the publisher. Such contracts usually specify that the dialog

> Precise placement of key words and phrases is critical on-stage.

---

3. Current copyright law extends the length of protection for any work created after 1976 until fifty years after the author's death. You wouldn't want to prematurely deprive your great-grandchildren of the royalty checks that will roll into your estate, now, would you?

may not be altered.

The prices of collectibles change even more rapidly. I made the mistake of mentioning the price of a collectable comic book in a play about fifteen years ago. I read through my play recently, and was curious as to what the current price might be. I posted a question about it on the Internet, and was quite surprised by the replies I received from people who deal in comics. What was worth $1,000 fifteen years ago is now worth over $80,000!

Word Placement And Order

Every thought that is put into words has some key element, a word or phrase that is the central idea being expressed. Where these key words are placed within the sentence or sentences that make up the thought determines how effectively the thought is communicated. If, for instance, you want to tell a child not to approach an animal that doesn't look too friendly, you would probably say something like: "Don't go near that dog! He might bite you. He looks dangerous. I don't think he wants to be petted."

The central idea—what you want communicated to the child —is placed right where it should be in this case. It's the first thing out of your mouth. All the rest merely presents reasons that back up the command: "Don't go near that dog!" If, however, you began with any of the other three sentences, the chances are the child might get himself bitten before you finished speaking.

In everyday speech, such concepts as placement of the words of the central idea being expressed never occur to the speaker. People say things exactly as the words come to them. In instinctive situations, such as the example just given, we usually get it right. Where there is no immediate danger to life and limb, however, we are much more lackadaisical in our approach to verbal communication. Words, sentences, concepts, etc. flow from our lips totally unfiltered and seemingly with no structure at all. There are no backspace or delete keys in the human brain (though there should be!). Nor is there a "cut and paste" function that edits the words that issue from our mouths. Misunderstandings frequently arise because of one person's failure to effectively communicate an idea to another. There is no room for such misinterpretations on-stage!

Unlike the denizens of Lewis Carroll's "Wonderland," your characters have to say what they mean and not just mean what they say. The lines of a play must be created so that there is no chance that their meaning can be misconstrued by the audience. If you try to duplicate street speech, the same possibility (and probability!) of being misunderstood exists in every line you create.

Precise placement of key words and phrases is critical on-stage. Carelessness in this area will result in confusion to the audience. If the central idea of a speech is lost because of poor placement, the speech has failed to do its job, and you as the playwright have failed to do your job.

This is particularly true when comedy is being written. You want the word or phrase that brings the laugh to come at the end of a line or at a point in the speech where a natural break occurs. Such a break would be a spot where the actor speaking the line can believably pause for as long as it takes for the audience to stop laughing.

There is a very good reason for this. People (it is hoped) will laugh as soon as they hear it. Laughter is spontaneous. It is not a commodity that is stored up and expended at some later time. If they are laughing, they cannot be *listening* to anything else being said on-stage. If your character continues speaking during the laughter, as he or she must if the key words that bring about the laugh come in the middle of a sentence that cannot be broken, one of two things will happen: (a) They will miss whatever else is said (undesirable). (b) They will stop laughing so that they do not miss what else is being said (even more undesirable!).

There are times when the improper placement of key words will kill a laugh altogether. To illustrate this let's look at a sequence I created for my play *Off With His Head*. In the opening lines of the first act, I have established one of the principals as a lady who has completely immersed herself in the world of spiritualism, sorcery, and enchantment. Her husband, a diehard non-believer, arrives home to find her chanting while staring into a bowl of water. She tells him she is using the bowl of water to focus her thoughts so she can communicate with the spirits. During their ensuing conversation, he makes a few pointed comments about "talking to bowls of water." I did this to set up the following laugh:

```
Harry: (Annoyed) I give up! (He moves
       toward the kitchen door.) I'll be in
       the kitchen if you want me.
Carol: I thought you said you were going out.
Harry: I changed my mind. There's a bowl
       of Jell-O in the refrigerator. I
       think I'll go have a chat with it!
```

The sequence of the lines as well as the word placement in Harry's last line are all essential to the eliciting the desired laugh. I first tell them that there is the bowl of Jell-O in the refrigerator. This is something anyone can quickly relate to and thus understand, but of itself, it is not funny. I *immediately* follow this with the line that I want them to laugh at: "I think I'll go have a chat with it!" *No other line follows this in the speech!* Further, note that the key words of the laugh line itself, "a chat with it," come at the end of the line. The audience does not have to stop laughing to listen to something else being spoken.

If I had written the speech like this: "I changed my mind. I think I'll go have a chat with the bowl of Jell-O that's in the refrigerator," I would have effectively killed the laugh, or at best, reduced it to a snicker. The reason is that the laugh brought out by the funny concept of chatting with the bowl of Jello would have been killed in mid-stream because the audience would have been simultaneously trying to assimilate the information that the Jell-O is in the refrigerator.

Another example: This, incidentally, is the Act Two curtain-falling laugh of my play *George Who?*. My protagonist, a teenage girl named Jan, has built a time machine in her basement.

In order to hide it from everyone, she has designed it so that the machinery is built into the walls of a closet and operates when a certain sequence of the room's light switches is pressed. The problem of the play is that she has unwittingly reached into the past and brought back the teenage George Washington. Her time machine is, unfortunately, a one-way device. She can't send him back to the eighteenth century. Since George is here in the present, he was not available to the Revolutionary War, which was lost because of this. Modern America is still a British colony.

By the end of the second act, Jan has finally figured out a way to reverse the effects of the time machine, but is still making tests to make sure that she can place George back exactly at the point in time he was extracted from. I created a second problem by having another girl in her class, a trouble-making busybody named Luella whom Jan detests, snooping around to see what Jan is up to. Through a series of events Luella has accidentally transported herself back to the 1700's. This occurred a few lines from the end of the act, and when Jan makes her final entrance of the act, she is unaware of what had happened. Here's her final speech:

```
Jan: Now, how did that switch get turned on?
     My goodness. With the room lights off,
     the time machine was activated. It's a
     good thing nobody was in the closet.
     It's all set to send George back.
     I wouldn't want to send anybody else
     back to 1748.
     (She faces the audience with a
     mischievous smile on her face)
     Except maybe Luella.
     (The Curtain Falls)
```

Once again, sentence sequencing and word placement is what makes this speech do exactly what I want it to—leave the audience laughing as the curtain falls. I first have two lines to establish Jan's surprise, then three to reinforce what has happened in the minds of the audience, a line to set up the laugh, and finally the laugh line. Any other arrangement would negate the laugh.

For the joke to work, the groundwork had to be first laid. I have to be sure that the audience is aware of what has happened while also being aware that Jan *isn't*. That's the purpose of the first five lines. Since there is nobody on-stage at the time to act as a straight-man to feed her the set-up to the laugh line, I had to have Jan do it herself. She does this with the line: "I wouldn't want to send anybody *else* back to 1748." Then, and only then, can I spring the punch line with any reasonable assurance that it will get the laugh I am looking for.

Since the joke itself revolves around sending Luella *back* into the past, I made sure that the *ends* of the two lines immediately preceding the punch line *gently* set the audience up for a gag centered around going back to 1748. This was done by precisely inserting the word "back" at the ends of both lines. Two left jabs, then the right cross to the chin for the knockout.

As I'm sure you've noticed, I've violated my own "three line rule" for a speech here. There are times when this is necessary. In this instance, Jan was the only one on-stage. If someone else was on with her, I could have had that person say one of the lines and broken the rest up into two speeches for Jan. Unfortunately, if anyone else were present on-stage at that point, the laugh would not work as well. What I did do, though, is make sure that the sentences were short and followed each other in a logical sequence. That way, the actress playing Jan should have no trouble learning the speech.

More about this particular method of building laughs as well as the various other ways humor works on-stage in the next chapter.

Chapter Ten

The Comedy In Amateur Comedies

F ar greater minds than mine have been trying to come up with a definitive explanation of humor since before the dawn of history. None have succeeded. So, I won't even bother to try. The truth of the matter is that while much is known about *what* makes us laugh, very little is known about *why*. Fortunately for writers of comedy, humor itself has been around even longer than the attempts to define it. Over the millennia, humankind has had the opportunity to observe a great many practical examples of the things that for some reason or other it finds funny. People have been laughing at the antics of other people, I suppose, ever since the first time two cavemen were out walking together and one of them accidentally stepped into a pile of mammoth poop.

It should be obvious that if you are going to be writing any kind of humor, you need to have a well-developed sense of humor yourself. Unless you have some sort of warped mentality[1], the things that make *you* laugh will almost certainly make others laugh too. So, it's simple. To write funny plays, just create dialog and situations that you find humorous. That's all there is to it, right? Not quite.

1.Don't worry; you don't. Purchasing this book was a definite indication of a healthy, sane, mature, logical, and thoroughly rational mind.

Understand this: A funny line or incident on-stage does not just happen. It is carefully crafted with much of the same meticulously honed skills that go into the writing of a fine and thoughtful line of poetry. We have already seen how sentence sequence and word order are vital components of a successful laugh line. Of equal importance is the work that goes into the construction of the joke. Just as a house or other building relies on a well-constructed foundation to stand on its own and not crumble to the ground, a hearty on-stage laugh depends on a solid foundation. It has to, if it expects to stand up to the vagaries of the diverse audiences it must play before.

Whichever of the two methods of writing dialog explained in Chapter Eight you choose to write your plays, there will come the time when you have to work on each funny sequence or laugh line to insure that it plays for maximum effectiveness.

Building A Laugh

There are many methods of building the foundation to an on-stage laugh. A well-written amateur comedy will employ several different techniques. It is never advisable to have each laugh in your play constructed similarly. This will result in your jokes and comic situations becoming predictable, anathema to any humor, on-stage or off. The secret is to know when to use a particular construction strategy, and of more importance, when *not* to.

I will be walking you through several of the more common ways to build a laugh. There are others, of course. In fact, some successful playwrights have developed their own singular approaches to the task. Others have used established techniques, but with twists that make them unique. That's what makes good comedy work—its fresh style.

The Aside

An *aside* is a fast and easy way to get a laugh. It consists basically of a line or lines that are spoken directly to the audience, rather than to others on-stage at the time. It provides an opportunity for one character to say anything he or she wants about another without the object of those comments being aware of what is being said. An aside can be as mild as a simple rebuke of sorts or as nasty as a sharp and pointed barb. It is rarely a compliment. Comic asides are most likely to be biting sarcastic remarks, since their object is to make the audience laugh.

The construction of an *aside* is quite simple because not much needs to be done to prepare the audience for it. The dialog spoken by the character who is the object of the aside usually provides all the motivation necessary for the sarcastic remark to be said to the audience. For example, imagine an on-stage situation where a somewhat overbearing wife is extolling the virtues of her father to a group of her friends in the Upstage Right area. Her husband is Left, a little further downstage than she is and is directing his comments to the audience.

```
Wife: Oh, yes. Daddy was a great influence
      on my life. In fact, people say we
      are very similar. We have the same
      attitudes, the same literary tastes,
      the same appreciation of the Arts.

HUSBAND: (Aside) The same mustache.
```

Reverse the situation. This time the husband is bragging to his buddies, and the wife is off to one side.

```
HUSBAND: Why did I marry her? Well, what else
         could I  do. She told me she adored me.
         She told me she worshipped the ground
         I walked on. She told me she couldn't
         live without me.
   WIFE: (Aside) She told him she was pregnant.
```

(The second example is just used for illustration. It is not the type of comment, funny though it may be, that should be included in a play for high school use. Recall that we want to stick with "G" rated material.)

While the aside is probably the easiest to construct technically, it is among the hardest to justify. That is, you need a *really* good reason to employ it. This is because an aside essentially has a character stepping outside the framework of the play and speaking directly to the audience. When this happens, the invisible fourth wall crumbles. The audience is no longer a detached body on the outside looking in. The actor is acknowledging their presence and drawing them into the action of the play.

Groucho Marx was the unparalleled master of the aside. So much so, that it became as much of his trademark as the cigar and painted mustache. He did it so well that most people in the audience thought he was ad-libbing whenever he did an aside, regardless of whether or not he was working with a scripted line that was intended to be spoken as an aside.

Unfortunately, it is a safe bet that none of the actors who will be performing your play will even approach the caliber of comedic excellence that Groucho had. So, you have to be careful when you ask them to perform a line that is an aside.

Whenever you utilize an aside, you will run less of a risk of having the person speaking it move "outside" the play if you set it up as more or less of a wise remark that he is saying to himself or herself. Both of the examples given could easily fall into this category if handled properly. That's why I specified that the actor delivering the aside be only slightly downstage of the rest of the actors. Resist the temptation to have the actor move to the extreme downstage area and "out of the picture" to deliver the line. Though he will be facing the audience as he says the line (the principal characteristic of an aside), he will still be well within the

> Understand this: A funny line or incident on-stage does not just happen.

proscenium and thus inside the frame created to keep the actors and set separated from the audience.

Asides can be done by both eccentrics and normals; however, eccentrics are the best characters to use asides believably. Once you establish a character as an eccentric, the audience will expect him or her to act, well...*eccentric*. And who would be more likely to talk to himself than an eccentric?

In the illustrations used, both characters speaking the asides are probably normals. (I'm not sure, though. I haven't written the rest of the play!) A normal can always get away with an aside as a one-shot deal. If, though, that character continually uses asides throughout the entire play, this fact alone might move him or her into the "eccentric" column, and some character adjustment might be necessary to keep the character believable.

One final word about asides. Avoid using long speeches that are to be done as asides. If you have someone routinely stepping outside the play with long speeches, that person becomes essentially a narrator in the mind of the audience. This will once again shatter the protection from the action of the play that the fourth wall provides.

The Sight Gag

Another easy way to get a laugh is by use of sight gags. A sight gag is anything that will make people laugh just by being observed by them, rather than as the result of a laugh line in the dialog. Sight gags run the gamut from laughable bits of costuming to tricky physical maneuvers by one character to hide something from another (though not from the audience, who are, of course, aware of what is being hidden and why it is being surreptitiously concealed).

Sight gags are always popular with amateur actors. It is nice not to have to depend on your timing and skill in the delivery of a line to get a guffaw or two from the other side of the footlights.

Some sight gags are built into the script of a play, while others depend on the imagination of the director and actors. That's why it is important to mix dialog-driven jokes of all types within the text of the play frequently. A successful comedy will never allow the audience to go too long without having a laugh for itself. The atmosphere of laughter is created in such a play, and once this is established, the house will be more inclined to laugh heartily at sight gags that they might otherwise merely snicker at.

A few quick examples of sight gags: I once played a comic version of a professional gambler cum gangster, who was the "heavy" in the show, albeit a laughable heavy. Two or three lines after my initial entrance, the dialog quickly established exactly who and what I was. I employed a black derby as part of my costume, and I inserted an ace of spades into the black ribbon hatband. I put it on the back side of the derby, and made sure that I kept my face forward so the ace remained unseen by the audience until I was ready to spring it on them. The opportunity presented itself about three minutes into my initial scene.

Sight gags are always popular with amateur actors.

A pretty girl wandered in from the wings and posed down center, preening and showing off her charms. It was right within the nature of my character to make an appreciative circle around her while she was posing. Doing so, of course, put my back to the audience as I moved in front of her. The audience was already giggling at the my comic lecherousness as I began circling her. As soon as the ace came into view, those giggles turning into a strong, sustained laugh.

This is the type of gag that is generated by the actor or director (although, I dare say, if the playwright had thought of it, he might have called for it in the script). I took advantage of a scripted sight gag as the curtain falling gag in my play *Vampires Are A Pain In The Neck*. This sight gag also provided me with the "Oh, no, here we go again" ending I was looking for.

Throughout the play, the protagonists had to deal with the antics of a visiting uncle from Transylvania, who just happened to be a vampire. Here's what happened at the end of the play, when they were sighing in relief because they had finally managed to get him and his "good friend" (a wolf-girl) out of the house and on their way back to the old country:

```
ALICE:  Do you think we've seen the last of them?
 PETE:  I'm sure of it.
ALICE:  Well, that's a relief. Do me a favor,
        Pete. Don't invite anymore of your relatives
        from Transylvania to our house.
 PETE:  (Nervously) Well, er...okay.
ALICE:  What's the matter?
 PETE:  My, er...cousin Frankie was due to
        arrive tonight, also.
ALICE:  (In horror) Cousin Frankie?
        (As if in answer to her suspicion, the front
        door bursts open and Cousin Frankie,
        who is, of course, the Frankenstein
        Monster- in full make-up —ENTERS,
        stumbles in his stiff gait toward
        downstage, as ALICE faints, falling into
        the armchair.)
                    CURTAIN
```

The only danger in employing sight gags is that if they occur too frequently, the entire play runs the danger of degenerating into slapstick, which is never desirable. Used judiciously, though, sight gags are an important addition to your repertoire of comedy.

The Running Gag

Running gags can be as simple as a single word or as complex as specific cadences in line sequences. The one characteristic that all running gags share is a *recognizable pattern of repetition*. Be forewarned, though: the jokes cannot be identical. There *must* be differences in each occurrence of a running gag or else it will be perceived (rightly so) as just a rehashing of the earlier joke. That will not work. What has to be repeated is the *form* of the joke. That is not to say that you cannot repeat words from one incidence to another. In most cases you have to; it is the pattern of the words or perhaps a key word or words that will trigger recognition in the audience.

In the musical comedy *The Apple Tree,* which had a Broadway run in the mid 1960s, a single word—brown—is not only a successful running gag, it is also the only connection between the three entirely different one-act plays that comprise the show. *And* it is used just once in each act! Moreover, it is used in a different context in each act; however, the audience never fails to recognize the connection. That is what you call a skillful utilization of a running gag!

In Murray Schisgal's hit Broadway comedy *Luv,* he made use of several running gags. Among the most memorable was a sequence that occurred just twice, once in each of the two acts. (This is enough to classify it as a running gag. It is the audience's recognition of the similarity that makes it so, not the number of appearances.) In these bits, two of the three actors in the play try to go one-up on another by giving comic examples of how deprived their childhood was. Here, it was the similarity of the cadence of the lines and the content of same rather than specific words that was utilized to successfully add a running gag to the show.

For a running gag to be successful, there must be continuity from act to act. Ideally, a running gag will appear twice in the first act, once in the middle of the second act, and a final time very close to the end of the third act. Further, the incidence of the two first act appearances of the running gag should be well spaced. If a running gag shows up much more frequently than that, two things will happen: the joke will become stale, hence boring, hence undesirable; and the audience may get the impression that the play is a one-joke show (very undesirable!).

In my play *George Who?* I turned an ordinary device, a ballpoint pen, into a running gag that sustained itself for the entire three acts. I used a slightly different running order, though. I introduced the idea in the middle of the first act but did not bring it back until Act Two. My George Washington character was not impressed by any of the wonders of the twentieth century such as electric lights, television, etc. What did make him stand up and take notice was—you guessed it—ballpoint pens! He was totally fascinated by the concept of a pen that didn't have to be continually dipped into an inkwell to work.

I reinforced the running gag with two widely separated second act references by George about his fascination with the device. When I finally returned him to his own time period at the end of the third act, I took advantage of my running gag by having my two protagonists, Jan and Lonnie, examine a set of United States postage stamps that featured a representation of the famous painting of the signing of the Declaration of Independence. There was an earlier humorous reference to this painting (making this *too* a running gag!) when George was still absent from the Revolutionary War (which was lost because of this). At that time, the stamps did not show people signing the Declaration; they showed them ripping it up! Here's how my dialog ran in the third act:

```
    JAN: I just thought of something.  The
         stamps — let's check them just to
         make sure.
         (She moves to the stamps, examines them.)
 LONNIE: Well, are they signing the Declaration
         of Independence?
    JAN: Yes, yes, they are...but wait
         a minute...
         (Holds stamps up for a closer look.)
         I don't believe this!
         (Picks up magnifying glass, examines
         the stamps with it.)
         Well, I'll be!  They're signing it
         with a ballpoint pen!
```

The Double Left Jab and Right Cross:

From the outset, let me say that you won't find the

term "Double Left Jab and Right Cross" in any book about on-stage comedy. The terminology is strictly my own; however, the concept is well-known and has been in use since long before I began my thirty-year-plus romance with the theatre.

Most of the heartiest laughs in your play will come from this type of gag. Consequently, it requires the most work on your part to be truly effective. While it is said that "the best laid schemes o' mice and men gang aft a-gley," a conscientious effort here on your part in planning the set-up for your punch line will inevitably come to welcome fruition for you in the form of sustained, robust laughter from your audience.

In use, this concept is an excellent example of the kind of work that goes into a carefully constructed laugh. If you are at all familiar with the sport of boxing, you will see how the building of this type of laugh is quite analo-gous to this stratagem in the ring. Basically, a fighter who wants deliver a potential knockout blow to his opponent will not just keep throwing right hand power punches to the head. If he did that, the other boxer would simply con-centrate his defensive moves on blocking each right hand thrown. In order to draw his defense away from protection against the right, the boxer throws several left jabs, punches that are not quite as powerful as the rights, but are nevertheless effective enough to require blocking by the opponent. Once the first pugilist has the second's con-centration focused on the incoming left jabs, he suddenly unleashes the right cross, the kind of powerful blow that could take him down for the count. Timed right, he catches the other by surprise and lands the blow flush on the chin.

The most effective laugh line to a joke of this nature is one that first has the audience properly set up for it and then lands with much the same surprise and power as the boxer's right cross. The secret is to plant the idea that is central to the joke in the audience's mind *without their realizing you are doing so*, reinforce it, and then, when they are figuratively looking in the other direction, slam home the punch line. The audience, like the boxer lying flat on the canvas, must never see the punch line coming. That's where the craftsmanship of the playwright comes in.

A great deal of subtlety is needed in your set-up dialog for this to work properly. You have to be ever mindful that your "left jabs" do not "telegraph" what the punch line will be. This will require several run-throughs in your head as well as several re-writes on paper for you to get the dialog just right. The "seed" has to be carefully planted (the first "jab"), shrewdly reinforced (the second "jab"), and then brought to fruition with the line that will get the laugh.

I would like to illustrate this, as well as several other points I have already covered in previous chapters by reproducing the opening dialog of my three act comedy *Go, Go, Go, UFO!*:

Right off the bat, I introduce two characters, Emily, a "normal" protagonist who is the mother of the family and Albert, her young son (an eccentric[2]). As the curtain opens, she discovers him dressed in a belted trenchcoat with an up-turned collar. He is systematically running his hands up and down the cracks of the front door. She sneaks up behind him and sticks a finger into his back.

```
      EMILY: Stick 'em up!
     ALBERT: (Jumping) Yipe!  (He realizes who it
             is, and turns.)  Ah, Ma, it's only you.
      EMILY: And who did you expect—Dr.
             Strangelove, maybe?
     ALBERT: Ma!
      EMILY: Albert, I don't mind you playing
             secret agent all day long, but I really
             don't think it's necessary for you to
             frisk our front door.
     ALBERT: I was looking for my telltale.
      EMILY: Your what?
     ALBERT: My telltale.  We secret agents use
             them all the time.  You see, I pluck
             one of my hairs and stick it across
```

2.Yes, children can be eccentrics. Remember, eccentric does not mean crazy, just unusual. If you look hard enough, you can find something unusual about any child! Sometimes, you don't even have to look too hard.

```
              the crack of the door. If it's missing
              when I return, I know somebody's
              come through the door.
     EMILY: You're pulling hairs out of your head?
              (She puts a hand on ALBERT'S shoulder.)
              Albert, children aren't suppose to
              pull their hair out—only parents.
```

Here, I have accomplished several things in the first nine speeches. I started with a small laugh on the very first line. In the second line, I've identified the two characters as mother and son. With the third, I was able to sneak in another small laugh. The fifth line has given a name to one of the characters, and has also established the basis for Albert's eccentricity (he is obsessed with becoming a secret agent).

The set-up for the jab, jab, and right cross type of laugh comes in the eighth line. I mention the word "hair." Notice that there is no warning that hair is going to be the basis of the laugh. The reinforcement comes in the first line of Emily's next speech, where hair is again mentioned. This is quickly followed by the punch line.

Observe that Albert's name is repeated once more two lines after it is first mentioned. This is enough to set the name firmly in the audience's mind. Since Emily is Albert's mother, I was not able to work her name in until a few pages later, as I could not have him calling his mother by her first name. But I did manage to have Albert refer to her as "Ma" twice at the outset, so the relationship is clear to the audience.

Another point that was established was the "secret agent" business. That, too, was mentioned twice in the opening dialog, as well as receiving reinforcement by the costuming I called for. So, several items of exposition are introduced gently by these speeches, as well as two small laughs and the first big laugh of the show. Not bad for nine lines, eh? (No applause please; send money.)

The set-up to this type of laugh line can also be accomplished with the cadence of the dialog, rather than through the repetition of specific words. Rhythmic patterns are as easily imprinted on the brain as repeated words.

Going back to my play *Vampires Are A Pain In The Neck*, for example, my primary eccentric, who is, as I mentioned earlier, the vampire[3] the title refers to, is mistaken for the husband of a woman who is trying very hard to be accepted into a snooty, upper-crust club called the Daughters of American Wealth.[4] When they arrive at the house and one of their number, Mrs. Snobbly, asks to see his wife, the following dialog ensues:

```
COUNT: You'll have to tell me which one of
       my wives you wish to see. Better still,
       why don't you describe her to me.
       I have so many brides, I tend to
       forget their names.
MRS. S: (Shocked) Do you mean to say that
       there is more than one Mrs. Von Bleck?
COUNT: Of course. I take new brides all the
       time. In fact, I think my nephew's maid
       will soon become my latest bride.
Mrs. S: (Now thoroughly shocked) Really,
       sir! I am shocked! (She takes a step
       closer to the COUNT) I am horrified!
       (She takes another step toward the
       COUNT, then stops) I am scandalized!
       (She is now only one foot from him.)
COUNT: Come any closer, and you will also
       be bitten!
```

As you can see, the three quick lines: "I am shocked." "I am horrified." "I am scandalized." form a rhythmic pattern that is echoed in the punch line : "...you will also be bitten." Here, I must admit, my left jabs number three. I have found that in using a cadence that consists of a quick, uninterrupted sequence of similarly

---

3. Vampirism is *quite* an eccentric trait. Wouldn't you agree?
4. The snootiness of each of the women in the club has been exaggerated by me to the point where each of them is also an eccentric.

114

sounding lines like those above, three jabs work even better than two. Remember - flexibility!

One Liners

While the double left jab, right cross joke may bring the strongest guffaws in a show, the one-liner is the device used most often to get a laugh. That is, the great majority of the gags in a humorous play are one-liners. Unlike other types of jokes, they don't require careful spacing within the acts or judicious use to avoid being boring. One-liners are, by their very nature, highly individual. They are not dependent on elaborate set-ups (though they *do* require some set-up, as will be explained) as do other types of gags. Therefore, they should be sprinkled quite liberally throughout a play. If you want to keep your audience laughing, you need to be constantly hitting them with your one-liners, sometimes one after another.

One-liners generally require only one set-up line to cue them. Sometimes the quick set-up for one comes from an action by an actor rather than from a line. In the previous example, the two smaller laugh lines were examples of one-liners. The very first speech of the show ("Stick 'em up!") is a one-liner that has been set up both by Albert's furtive movements around the door and Emily's jabbing of her finger into his back. The second, the "Dr. Strangelove" quip was set up by a perfectly innocuous straight line: "Aw, Ma, it's only you."

> The one-liner is the device used most often to get a laugh.

You do have to be careful with your one-liner set-ups. Unlike the more intricate set-ups required by other jokes, you usually only have that single straight line or action to work with. Consequently, you must employ the most potent tool in the playwright's bag of verbal tricks, word order, when the set-up is another actor's line. Make sure nothing comes between the operative word or words of the straight line and the one-liner.

For example, if Albert's line had been: "Aw, Ma, it's only you. You scared me," those extra three words would have made Emily's line much less effective in bringing about the desired laugh. Read these two lines both ways, and you will see what I mean.

Let's take a look at a one-liner from my play *Heavy Metal!*. Here I have a family moving into their new home. The husband, Bob, has just lugged an extremely heavy box in from the moving truck and has plopped it down heavily on a table.

> KATHY: Be careful, Bob. I have china in
> those boxes.
> BOB: (Plops himself into downstage chair
> of table and massaging the muscles
> in his arms.) It feels like you have
> half of Japan in there, too!

The operative words of Kathy's straight line feed are: "china in those boxes." If she had added: "You'll break my plates." or something along those lines, the set-up would have been completely ruined. To return to the boxing analogy we used earlier, this would be similar to a fast "one-two" punch. Verbally, that's exactly how it has to be delivered! Straight line, gag line—wham, bam. Just like the boxer's one-two shots, your one-liners, if delivered properly, will land home solidly! And your play will be a knockout!

One-liners can follow each other in rapid succession to keep the laughter rolling in much the way a stand-up comic hits the audience with one quick joke after the other. In the following dialog from my play *Alias (MS) Santa Claus*, my very unconventional Saint Nick, an eccentric, is speaking to the protagonist, Christine, a normal who plays straight man for the series of gags.

> CHRISTINE: Do you mean to tell me *The Night*
> *Before Christmas* isn't accurate?
> NICK: It's wrong from beginning to end.

```
                 For instance, I don't live at the
                 North Pole; I live in Northport.
                 And all that business about sleds and
                 reindeer—sheer nonsense!
CHRISTINE: Oh, no.  Don't tell me you don't
                 have a sleigh with eight tiny reindeer?
     NICK: Are you kidding?  I have a Buick
                 with a stick shift and eight very large
                 cylinders.
CHRISTINE: You make all of your Christmas
                 deliveries by car?
     NICK: Most of the time. If the load is
                 too heavy, I use a rent-a-truck.
```

Exaggerations and Intentional Mispronunciations

A laugh-generating technique that works quite nicely when used by your eccentrics, is exaggeration. You will remember that one of the ways to establish the eccentricity of a character is to exaggerate his or her traits. This exaggeration can be carried over to dialog spoken by or about the character.

The exaggeration should be something that is way beyond what a normal person would do, but not to the extent that it would move from the realm of the improbable to that of the impossible. If, for example, you wanted to portray a person as a total computer fanatic, you might have a bit of dialog that goes like this:

```
A: Just how many computers do you own, anyway?
B: How many?  Gee, I lost count about ten
   gigabytes ago. Let's see, there's four
   in the living room, six in the bedroom,
   two in the kitchen, and five in the basement.
   Oh, I almost forgot the one in the bathroom.
A: How could you possibly use a computer
   in the bathroom?
B: It's a laptop.
```

You have to admit that eighteen computers are more

than one person could possibly need, and certainly more than anyone you or I know owns. But while it is a laughable amount, it also *is not beyond belief.* If, on the other hand, the dialog indicated that he had *seven hundred* computers in the house, it would be completely unbelievable, and consequently would get more of a groan than a laugh from the audience. Also, there probably would be a few more empty seats in the house after the next intermission.

In the example given, the exaggeration serves more as a buildup to the laptop joke, but the exaggeration itself can become part of the punch line to a gag. Let's return for a moment to Jan and Luella from my play *George Who?*. Luella, the busybody, is also the local high school glamour girl. In a discussion with Jan about all the different boys she has gone steady with, the following dialog occurs:

```
    JAN: What's your definition of going steady,
         anyway— dating the same boy twice?
 LUELLA: I never have to wait that long.
         Boys always ask me to go steady on the
         first date.
    JAN: And you accept, of course.
 LUELLA: Certainly. I wouldn't want to
         disappoint the dear boys. They're so
         sweet when they offer me their class
         rings, and I know how it would break
         their hearts if I said no, so naturally
         I accept. After all, Noblesse Oblige.
    JAN: You must have quite a collection of
         class rings.
 LUELLA: One hundred and sixty-seven, to be
         exact. I've had to take out a safe
         deposit box at the bank.
```

Both examples above consist of an exaggeration gag by the character himself or herself. Exaggeration jokes about one character by another will also bring a good-sized laugh. The person who speaks the dialog should be in a position to know about the things she is talking about rather than just speculating about something she is not in a position to know.

In the following clip from my play *Go, Go, Go, UFO!*, the object of the exaggeration is Emily's husband and Marie's father. Glenda is not related, and serves as a straight man (woman?) for the gags that ensue.

```
  MARIE: Do you remember how my bed used to
         sag in the middle?  Well, now it doesn't
         anymore, it bulges. Dad has piles of
         science fiction magazines stacked up
         under it.
  EMILY: Oh, no!  And he promised to leave
         your room alone after that business
         last summer. You haven't tried to open
         your closet door, I hope.
  MARIE: Are you kidding?  (To GLENDA) The
         last time my father started using my
         room as a warehouse, I went looking in
         my closet for jogging shoes and ended
         up buried alive under a pile
         of paperbacks.
 GLENDA: My goodness. Were you hurt?
  MARIE: Nothing worse than a few broken
         fingernails from clawing my way up to
         the surface.
 GLENDA: But why does your father stuff your
         closet with books in the first place?
  MARIE: It's his hobby.
 GLENDA: Stuffing closets?
  MARIE: No.  Collecting science fiction.
  EMILY: Bill has an uncontrollable passion
         for science fiction. He has just about
         every book and magazine that's been
         published in the field. The trouble is,
         he never throws any of them away. He
         keeps them all in the house.
 GLENDA: Well, I guess every man needs a
         hobby, but why does he insist on storing
```

```
              his books in your daughter's room.
              Don't you have an attic?
       EMILY: He filled the attic up years ago,
              along with the game room, all six spare
              bedrooms, and the tool shed out back.
              I haven't checked out the barbecue
              pit yet.
```

Intentional mispronunciation (by the playwright) can also be a source of laughs. Unlike exaggeration, however, this is more suited to your normal characters, and is used because they can believably be unfamiliar with what they're talking about. Make sure, though, that the audience is familiar with the term, or there is no point to attempting to use it as a joke. In addition, the jokes will be funnier if the mispronunciation is actually another, totally unrelated word.

Here are two lines from a new play I am currently working on:

```
      AURORA: (With folded arms)  You and your
              little side-kick had better not be
              up to any highjinks with that computer
              of yours. I have read about the
              trouble you young computer hagglers
              get into.
    SAMANTHA: That's "hackers," Aunt Aurora.
```

Another two-line example from my play *Murder Most Fowl* finds Watson desperately trying to review material for a medical school test[5]:

```
      WATSON: Now, let's see...first there's
              the esophagus which leads to the
              stomach. The there's the duodenum...Oh,
              can't forget the liver and gall
              bladder and that thing that
              starts with a "p"...er...the pantheon
```

---

5. In this spoof, my Watson, you see, is not a doctor yet.

```
        or the panatella or...

    JONES: (Stops pacing, faces Watson) A
           panatella is a cigar, Watson.
```

The Exit Line Laugh

As playwrights, we share an analogous ultimate goal with those mighty ring warriors I have been comparing our efforts to. The professional fighter wants to leave his opponent reeling on the canvas. The professional writer of amateur comedies wants to leave his audience rolling in the aisles. And like our pugilistic counterparts, playwrights should never hesitate to throw a sucker punch if the opportunity arises.

Oddly enough, the opportunity to throw a good "sucker punch" makes itself available quite frequently. It happens whenever a character makes an exit. The object of both the physical and verbal "sucker punch" is to catch the intended recipients when their guard is down. The audience does not expect to hear anything else from an actor on his or her way offstage. If a boffo laugh line erupts from actors on their exit, it will have a much greater impact than if said in the course of normal on-stage dialog.

When I say "on their exits," I don't mean to imply that the line should be directed into the wings while the actors are physically stepping offstage. Any comedic value of the line would, of course, be lost if done that way. Moreover, the line itself would probably not even be heard, as it would be attenuated to a whisper by all the curtains and other sound-absorbing materials associated with a stage set.

Rather, the exit line is delivered to another actor (or to the audience if it is also an aside) *just before* the actor speaking it takes the final steps that will carry him or her offstage. This means that the audience must be aware that the actor is about to exit. Generally, there is no need to hang out a flag that announces a character's imminent exit. In the normal course of the dialog within a well-constructed scene, it should become apparent that an actor is preparing to exit.

Special cases exist, of course. There are times when a sudden exit is an intricate part of the plot. Moreover, an unexpected exit might be turned into a humorous situation in itself. For instance, whenever a character must quickly hide, either on-stage or off, the opportunity for a humorous situation, with or without accompanying dialog, arises.

What we are concerned with here, though, are the instances where it is obvious that a character is going to make an exit from the stage. This usually occurs only a few lines from the actual exit, so we do not have a lot of time to set up the gag. In fact, extra care needs to be taken here not to alert the audience to the upcoming laugh line, since we want to sucker-punch them.

Let's take a glance at an example of how this works. Throughout the entire first scene of my play *Heavy Metal!*, I had been taking advantage of the eccentricity of my character, Grandpa, for laughs both by him and about him. Grandpa is the "mad scientist" whose experiments inevitably blow up, taking all or part of the house with them. Peter, his grandson, is Grandpa's major ally. He wants to become a scientist also. Consequently, he is the one person in the family who knows the most about Grandpa's work. With the family's move into a new house, both Peter's Mom and Dad are concerned about the equipment Grandpa is bringing in with him. Peter has been reassuring them that everything brought in is safe. All of this has set the stage for the following laugh on one of his exits. As we join the scene, Kathy, Peter's mother, is speaking to him. She is asking him to go out and help his father bring in a piece of furniture.

```
KATHY: You'd better go help him with that bed.
       I'm going to go sweep up whatever
       it was those movers dropped upstairs.
       Of course I have to find my
       brooms first.
PETER: They're in the broom closet.
       I put them there myself.
KATHY: This house has a broom closet?
PETER: Sure. It's right over there.
```

```
(Indicates broom closet)
I discovered it while I was looking
for a place to store Grandpa's
portable atom smasher.
(EXITS through front door.)
```

The audience knows that Peter is about to exit through the front door since his mother has asked him to help his father take the bed from the moving van. Three lines occur before the actual exit. Two are innocent enough; they are concerned with the broom closet. The audience is lulled by these. They are expecting him to exit without further ado. The final line, just before he steps offstage is my sucker-punch. The gag about the portable atom smasher hits them without warning!

In my play *Go, Go, Go, UFO!* I have an eccentric who is the quintessential nosy neighbor. She is forever finding excuses to enter the protagonist's house and snoop around. She arrives with a cup in hand on the pretext of borrowing a cup of sugar. This is the dialog that ensues just before Emily (the protagonist) exits to her kitchen to get the sugar:

```
       EMILY: I'll get your sugar so you
              can leave.
              (She turns and heads for the
              kitchen doorway).
MRS. PINCUS: Wait a minute. You forgot the cup.
       EMILY: (Pausing and turning back.) I
              don't need it, I'm going to give you
              the whole bag.
MRS. PINCUS: But I only need a cup.
       EMILY: I know, but you can keep the
              bag anyway. That way, the next ten
              times you need to come over and
              borrow a cup of sugar from me, you
              can do it without coming over!
              (She turns and EXITS)
```

Emily's move toward the kitchen and her line about getting the sugar serves notice that she is about to exit. Here, I combine my double left jab tactic with my fast sucker-punch. I mention the word "cup" twice, setting it in the audience's mind, even though their natural instinct is to dismiss this as just dialog to get the character offstage. Little do they know that they're being set up for the sucker-punch on that exit. *Heh, heh.*

Playwrights should never hesitate to throw a sucker punch if the opportunity arises.

Chapter Eleven

Miscellaneous Play Creation Topics

Stage Directions

As I'm sure you've noticed, excerpts from my own published plays cited within the previous chapters contain more than just the words spoken by my characters. The various stage directions that are required are also included along with the dialog.

Stage directions are an integral part of any play. After all, a production is not merely a recitation of lines. Actors must enter, exit, and move about the stage as the scenes come to life. Not all stage directions, however, originate with the playwright. In fact, most do not. Recall my earlier statement: "The production of any play is a collaboration between playwright, director, and actor." Each has a job to do if a show is to be successful. Yours is to write the dialog that is to be spoken on-stage. The actors' job is to interpret your dialog in such a manner as to breathe life into the characters they are portraying. The director has not one, but rather two jobs. The first is to bring focus to the entire production, to coordinate the work of his fellow collaborators (you and the actors) into a cohesive production. The second is to move the players around the stage in a logical, believable, and effective manner.

It is important to understand this. The majority of stage directions for your play will come from the various directors who will be in charge of individual productions of it, *not from you.* Your function is to provide only the stage directions that are *absolutely essential* to the understanding of your play. Entrances and exits obviously fall into this category. *Significant*[1] character emotions and responses (anger, joy, surprise, fear, hesitancy, etc.) to be incorporated into the speaking of a given line should also be included. Certain lines can be interpreted in several different ways. It is helpful for the director to know what you had in mind when you wrote a speech that can be played in several different ways.

I have already addressed the times that specific character movements are required for the set-up to a given joke. Encompass these movements within your script. *All other movement falls with the purview of the director!*

If you call for every bit of blocking necessary for the production of your play within the script, one of several things (all counter-productive) will happen. For openers, you will have severely limited the director's ability to respond to the individual needs of his or her production. Plays are produced on stages of all sizes and configurations. Your blocking may prove to be awkward for the set that is being used. If the director feels obliged to follow your stage directions, the production will most likely come off in a clumsy manner. Other directors may choose to ignore *all* of the pre-printed blocking because there is so much of it. This leads to an even bigger problem. It means that the movement set-ups you have carefully orchestrated for some of your gags will be lost along with the rest.

Since you are writing for the high school market, many of the people who will be directing your plays will not be seasoned, veteran directors. In schools that have a Drama Department, one of the drama coaches will undoubtedly get the assignment, so your play will usually be

---

1. Not all lines carry significant emotions. Most do not. Don't try to direct the productions of your play from behind your monitor screen by including an emotion for each line spoken. If you are addicted to crossword puzzles, as I am, you may recall that a clue that reads "Overact" or "Ham it up," usually is for the word "emote."

in safe hands. Be aware, though, such veteran directors scrupulously ignore printed stage directions from the playwright if they are too voluminous.

Most high schools, unfortunately, do not have a Drama Department *per se*, so the task will inevitably be handed over to one of the English Literature instructors. While such teachers have much theoretical knowledge of drama, having studied the classics in college, they usually do not have a great deal of practical experience with actual play production. Inexperienced directors are more apt to follow printed stage directions closely. A production can very quickly become tied up in knots if the director tries to follow every printed stage direction to the letter in scripts that are overly laden with them. By keeping the directions in your script to a minimum, you will actually be doing them *and* the school a enormous service. By forcing them to tap their creative potential in order to move their actors around the stage, you will be helping them to learn the art of play direction. Subsequent productions directed by the same people will just keep getting better and better!

Never write a stage direction that will force an actor to upstage himself.

One further comment about stage directions. Never write a stage direction that will force an actor to upstage himself or another actor. This is another reason to keep stage directions to a minimum in your script. There are some things that just cannot be entirely envisioned in your head as you write the play. One of them is the locations of all the actors on the stage at any given moment. The director is in a much better position to see this.

If you look back at the dialog involving Mrs. Pincus and her cup of sugar mentioned in the previous chapter, you'll see that I have Emily pausing in her movement toward the kitchen doorway and moving back to Mrs. Pincus before responding to the line: "Wait a minute. You forgot the cup." There is a good reason for this. In the set I designed for this show, the front door (where Mrs. Pincus is standing) is along the upstage wall, and the kitchen doorway is down right. If Emily continued toward the kitchen, or even stopped where she was to deliver her line, she would have had to turn her back to the audience and upstage herself to deliver the line.

Emily's movement toward the kitchen is needed, as it is part of the set-up for the joke. That's why it was included. Since I established the blocking for this move, I had the responsibility of making sure that I didn't put the director in an untenable position by writing stage directions that would hamper the delivery of the punch line. Anytime you incorporate stage direction into your dialog, you incur a similar responsibility. Another reason to leave most of the blocking to the director!

Lighting and Sound Effects

For the most part, the playwright need not be concerned with the lighting of his or her play. The technical aspects of providing sufficient light for the show are the responsibility of the lighting director for any given production, while calling for the artistic use of lighting effects (for setting moods, etc.) falls within the province of the director. The only lighting cues you should be specifying in your script are those which indicate blackouts (very useful for indicating the passage of time without closing the act curtain) or the dimming/ brightening of the set for reasons that are part of the plot. Probably the best known dramatic use of such dimming and brightening of the lights by the playwright occur in the play *Angel Street*, which you may be more familiar with under the movie title *Gaslight*.

Unlike lighting cues, it is necessary for the playwright to indicate *most* of the sound effects in the script. Generally these are not spectacular effects such as bombs exploding or airplanes making low passes, but are the rather mundane sounds of telephones or doorbells ringing, doors slamming offstage, and the like. The timing of such effects within the scope of a play is not arbitrary or open to artistic interpretation. They must occur on specific lines. The only exceptions would be ambient sounds added for a more realistic production. An outdoor scene, for instance, might be enhanced by judicious use of birds calls in the background.

Both lighting and sound cues that are included in the text of the play should also be listed in sequential order on separate lighting and sound sheets. See the chapter on manuscript format for exactly what such sheets should look like. It is important to record these cues on their own sheets as soon as you create them. That is one of the reasons you should be using a word processor that allows you to keep multiple documents open at the same time. You can simply block the text describing the effect and the cue for it in your main script file and copy it over to the appropriate page. You will have to format the copied text in a slightly different manner on your cue sheets, but you will be saved from the task of re-typing it.

In addition, as you work on the script, you should keep open the file that records all props, whether on-stage or personal, and note them in that file (see the chapter on manuscript format for an example of what this sheet should look like) as soon as they appear or are brought on-stage. Once again, this will prove to be a tremendous time saver when you are assembling all the miscellaneous information that must be submitted along with your text of the dialog.

Backing Up Your Work

Do yourself a great favor and do a daily backup of each of the computer files associated with your play. Make at least two copies from the hard drive onto floppy disks and store them in different locations. One trick I use frequently is to stash one backup disk in the briefcase I take back and forth to my day job[2]. This way, I don't have to start again from scratch in case of fire, natural disaster, or theft at home while I am away at work.

Store your backup disks away from any source of heat (radiators, hot plates, etc.) or magnetism. This includes not

---

2. Yes, you need a day job. Writing plays for amateurs is a nice source of extra income, but I don't know of anybody who was able to live solely on the revenue it produces.

only the obvious, magnetic clips and note holders, but also anything that generates electromagnetic waves. Don't, for example, keep them on top of, or even too close to, your stereo speakers. Be especially carefully not to place them, even temporarily, next to or under a telephone. One ring could wipe out the data on a disk.

While I am a great proponent of soft documentation, I would also urge to you keep a hard copy of your completed pages in a looseleaf binder. This serves several useful purposes. It is an emergency backup of your many hours of hard work, one that cannot be destroyed by hard disk failure or magnetic waves and is not likely to be stolen. Moreover, the hard copy provides an easy-to-read reference for you when you need to quickly check on things like who was on-stage when a certain line was said or how long one character or another has been offstage.

Keeping Things Straight

Refer to your hard copy frequently. I do a complete read through of it every ten pages or so. Since you are creating a work designed to be viewed all at once in the short span of a few hours, and are writing it over a period of months, inconsistencies will arise. Very few of us have the type of photographic memory that will allow us to recall instantly every entrance, exit, and bit of dialog spoken by our characters.

Well maintained character sheets will help you keep discrepancies in such things as ages, relationships, et al. from cropping up; however, you will have to supplement this by continually checking over your completed pages. You may discover that you have Aunt Agatha going off to bed at one point and then showing up at the front door on her way back from a trip to the mall a dozen pages later. Or that an off-stage character referred to as "Uncle Stefan" in Act One has mysteriously become "Uncle Stephen" in Act Two.

In addition, you may find that what seemed to pour forth from your keyboard as the perfect bit of dialog last week looks a little lame now that it's had a chance to "mature." Don't be afraid to edit and re-edit as often as necessary in order to make your words sparkle with theatrical brilliance.

There will be times when large segments of dialog from one act need to be undergo serious revision or even be eliminated[3] due to a twist you have come up with in a later second act. Allow me to repeat this for the umpteenth time: play creation is a *dynamic* process. Nothing is carved in stone except the words on a grave marker[4]. Allow yourself to go with the flow of your creative process.

Titling Your Play

Titling a play is practically an art in itself. There will always be several possible names for any given play. Most of the titles you think up will be adequate. A few will be exceptional. Only one, however, will be the ultimate *mot juste* for the dramatic work you have created. Finding that one title among the many that will present themselves to your imagination is a task that you should devote some time to.

A catchy name will not, in itself, sell a poorly written play, but a well-though-out, witty title *will* enhance the salability of a good script many times over. Since the success of your play depends entirely upon how often it is produced, you obviously want as many producers as possible to read through the catalog listing for it. And the play's title will always be the salient feature in any publisher's catalog blurb. It is always set in a large, eye-catching font to attract prospective producers to the listing.

Refer to your hard copy frequently.

One of the criteria I set for myself in selecting a name for my plays is the "Rule of Five." I seldom use more than five words to name my play. In my opinion, the ideal title is

---

3. Don't ever completely erase blocks of dialog. Keep a ongoing "discard" file somewhere on your hard drive. Copy any cohesive blocks of dialog that you no longer need for your play in this file. Put some sort of separator between these (two or three blank lines will do). Glance through this file when you are in need of inspiration for your next play. You may be able to build an entire play around something that was well-written, but just didn't work out in your current effort.

4. I plan to have my own read: "At last — a plot!"

only two words long. Three is okay, four is pushing it, and five is the absolute most. Single word titles are usually more appropriate for musicals (*Oklahoma!, Carousel, Mame, Showboat, Cabaret, Cats,* and so forth).

Titles of more than five words are cumbersome to all who have to advertise the play, starting with the publisher who has to squeeze the words into what he hopes will be an attractive catalog listing. It also becomes a problem for the producers of your play who have to fit it on one line of the programs, posters, ads, etc.

Here are a few possible avenues to explore when searching for the right title for your play. Puns and other plays on words are always popular. A few examples from popular plays are Sir Noel Coward's *Blithe Spirit*, and Oscar Wilde's *The Importance Of Being Earnest.* Titles that give new meaning to cliche phrases such as *My Fair Lady* or *Black Comedy* also work well. Literary references such as George Bernard Shaw's *Arms and The Man* and *Pygmalion* can be effective; however, you should be aware that they may be lost on today's media-heavy world where reading has almost become a lost art and the reading of classics is a lost art. A better choice here might be phrases that are recognizable to most people (Some examples from the professional stage would be *Light Up The Sky, Once In A Lifetime,* and *Your Own Thing*).

One word of caution: If your publisher does not like your title, be flexible enough to accept this. You will probably be asked to come up with several alternates for her to choose from in such an instance. Do yourself a favor and do as she requests. Don't lose a sale over as pretentious an issue as "artistic integrity." If you have hit on the perfect title, chances are that she won't request another title; however, if she does, be wise enough to defer to her judgement. She knows what will sell. Trust her!

Getting Produced

Many publishers of plays for amateur use prefer that a new play has undergone at least one production before they consider it for inclusion in their catalog. This is not *absolutely* necessary, as most publishers are aware that new playwrights might not be associated with local producing companies of amateurs, but if you can get your play produced, it is very much in your interest to do so for several reasons that I will outline.

Since this book is being written for writers who are new to the field of playwriting, I will explain some of the ways you can locate and approach the amateur troupes and high school drama depart-ments in your area, but first let me tell you the ways a production can help make your script an even better and more saleable commod-ity on the market.

Do not offer to direct the play.

One of the pricipal purposes of seeking pre-publication production for a new script is prob-lem location. No matter how experienced in playwriting and theatre in general you may be, you can never *entirely* spot ev-ery problem a play might have until you see it being acted out on-stage.

There may be, for instance, lines that appeared to be speakable on a single breath when you wrote them, but do cause a big problem for whichever actors must speak them. Some might actually be tongue twisters, particularly if you are fond of alliteration[5]. You might also find that a character does not have enough time between exiting and re-entering to make a required costume change. In addition, you may discover that despite your careful attention to the on-stage population at all times, you have a character standing around doing and saying nothing for too long a stretch. All of these problems and many more will become evident once a play goes into production. Dead or inordinately slow spots in your play will also show themselves, sometimes in places where you thought your script was exceptionally tight.

Chances are that your play will not have all of these difficulties, but I can guarantee that it will have some of

5. If you are, use it sparingly!

them. Why? Because of the vast difference in perspective that exists between staring at a typewriter or computer monitor and actually seeing the dynamics of dialog in action on a stage. I personally have over thirty years experience in theatre, most of those years as a playwright (in addition to acting, directing, producing, etc.), and I have never once gone through a pre-publication production of one of my plays without having done at least some re-writing of the script. That's why many publishers would like you to do likewise.

Since your play has been specifically designed for high school use, the first places you should approach in your quest for pre-publication production would be the high schools in your area. If you live close enough to your old alma mater, start with that school. Doing a play written by an alumnus or alumna always presents the school with an opportunity to sell more tickets, and you can bet it will be a point that receives prominent notice in their advertising. Another big selling point is the fact that they will be able to do your show without payment of a royalty. Do not even think of asking for a royalty, by the way. They are doing a great service to you by giving your play a production. Don't forget that.

Do *not* offer to direct the play. The teachers who usually direct student productions will resent an "outsider," even one who is a member of the alumni, intruding upon their "territory." It may knock your play out of contention for selection. In addition, it is very necessary to have someone who will not be protective of "their baby" to the detriment of the show as a whole in charge of the production. If serious problems with the script exist, an experienced director will be in a much better position than you to spot them. Also, he or she may be able to offer you some sound advice on how to solve them. Do make yourself available at all times as a consultant to the production. Try to attend as many rehearsals as possible. What you should *not* do is make your presence a source of annoyance to the director with constant interruptions or any show of moodiness if you are not happy with something he or she is doing. With the exception of million-dollar prima donna movie and television "stars," the legendary theatrical artistic "temperament" is a myth. The truth is that there are too many talented people and too few positions for actors, directors and playwrights to go around. There will always be someone equally as gifted available to quickly replace anyone who is stupid enough to display temperament.

If you are unable to convince a high school (or junior high) to produce your play, you could look into the various community theatre companies in your area. They can be easily located by checking the "Community Events" calendars of your local newspaper. Community theatres historically have very little budget for advertising, and the "Community Events" section of local papers is a readily available source of *free* advertising.

Keep copies of all promotional material from the production of your show.

While such companies usually look for tried-and-true material, they may be amenable to producing your play for many of the same reasons as local high schools, i.e., no royalties and the opportunity to push the fact that this is a new comedy by a local playwright.

If a community theatre group does agree to do your show, you might have to do some re-writing of the script to eliminate some of the superfluous characters (those one or two line or walk-on parts stuck in for the larger cast needs of high schools). Be willing to do so for the sake of this production, but be sure to re-insert them when you submit your script to publishers. Most of the problems with your play that production will bring to light will not involve these extra cast members, so your work will still benefit from being staged by a community group.

Keep copies of all promotional material from the production of your show, including programs, flyers, publicity kits, and so forth. In addition, clip any favorable reviews from local newspapers. Prepare a neatly organized package of this material, and send it to potential publishers along with your manuscript. It will greatly enhance your chances of making a sale!

If you are unable to have a production of your play mounted, you might consider a public reading of the text. For this, I would once again suggest contacting one of the community theatre groups in your area. A good time to interest them in such a project would be when they are between shows. Some community groups go from the closing of one show right into production for the next, but most limit their efforts to twice a year (usually in the May-June or October-November time frame).

A public play reading provides a good opportunity for the members of the troop to get together between shows without the commitment of time necessary when going into production. In most cases, a single night's effort is all that is required. The actors involved will usually have enough experience to do justice to the script, even as a cold reading.

> **Anything you write is *automatically copyrighted* the minute you create it!**

Your "audience" for this reading will most likely be composed of actors in the troop who are not reading, along with as many of your friends as you can muster together. You should also invite the public to the reading. If you don't charge an admission fee to the public (which is never advisable for a reading) and advertise with flyers and a mention in the "Community Events" of your local paper, you will probably attract several senior citizens and other people who don't get out much. A copy of your flyers or a snipping of the newspaper mention will serve as proof to potential publishers that such a reading occurred.

Be prepared to take notes at your public reading. Listen to and watch the audience carefully. Fidgeting is a good indication that the particular section of the script being read at the time is becoming boring and is need of revision. In addition, you can see which comic lines are working and which fall flat. Again, close examination of jokes that fail to bring a laugh is in order. Perhaps the build-up to the laugh is wrong or the timing of the lines is off. As I have already explained, certain types of gags require physical movement by the actors and so will not go over as well during a reading. There is also the possibility (cough, cough) that the line is not as funny as you thought it might be. Don't be afraid to revise based on the reactions you get to your script. After all, the honing of the dialog based on the results of a performance or public reading is precisely the reason that many publishers suggest one or the other before submitting your script to them.

Copyright Protection and Your
Unpublished Manuscript

If you do elect to produce your play before submitting it to prospective publishers, you will need to reproduce copies of the script for the actors and other members of the crew to work with.

Naturally, the question of protecting your work from unauthorized use or outright theft when unpublished copies are in circulation comes up in such a case.

Fortunately, the revisions to the US copyright laws that were made in 1977 and 1989 come to your rescue here. In the past (prior to 1978), production of a play constituted a publication of sorts, and failure to secure a copyright registration prior to the performance of the script or failure to print a notice of this registration in any distributed copy could possibly throw it into the public domain, which means that anyone could use it without any payment whatsoever to the author. Be assured that this is no longer the case. Now, copyright protection is automatic *even before registration of the work has been secured!*

Anything you write (or key into your computer) is *automatically* copyrighted *the minute you create it!* Published or unpublished, you are protected by copyright. Moreover, the copyright, as has been mentioned earlier in this book, extends the length of your life plus an additional fifty years.

Your eventual publisher will secure a registered copyright for the published edition of your play, but until your play is published, you can obtain copyright protection for your script merely by claiming that you are the copyright holder on any copies of it. Here's all that needs to appear on the bottom of the first page: "Copyright (Author's name)." The year does not even have to be mentioned on unpublished works (as of March 1, 1989).

There are definite advantages that a registered, published edition of any work has over the protection afforded an unpublished, unregistered work (but still copyrighted because the author has given notice to the world that he or she is the owner!), but in general, you should not need to worry yourself over them while your play is being produced as an unpublished work.

Chapter Twelve

The One-Act Play

Although the primary needs of most publishers who lease plays to amateurs are for full-length plays, they do include some shorter, one-act plays in their catalogs. One-act scripts (usually 30-45 minutes playing time, occasionally up to an hour's length) are used by amateur troupes for a variety of reasons. In some cases, the performance of the play is part, but not all, of an evening's entertainment, such as a short play that is included in the program for a Christmas "Family Night" at a school or church. There are also times when an amateur group may elect to produce a show made up of two or three one-act plays, rather than one full-length play. Another use for plays in the one-act format is for play contests, where several amateur groups compete against each other.

In any case, the process of creating one-act plays for amateur use is similar in many ways to that of full-length plays; however, there are several significant differences. Some of these differences make the writing of a one-act play easier than its "big brother," the three-act play. In many ways, though, this format is actually harder to work with. That's why I have spent so much time in this book helping you to master the creation of plays in the three-act format before even discussing shorter scripts. Let's take a look at some of those similarities and differences.

The Idea

Coming up with a workable idea for a one-act play is accomplished in exactly the same manner as for a full-length play. In fact, this is the stage of creation where you will probably decide (as do I) whether or not any given idea can sustain itself for three acts or if it should be become the basis of a one-acter. Some ideas, you will find, natu-rally lend themselves to development that will extend to three acts. Others will peter out after a single act, and if you try to stretch them into the longer format they will show defi-nite signs of this stretching.

> The idea for a one-act play should begin with an "unusual event" or "unusual character."

The idea for a one-act play should begin, as it does for full-length plays, with an "unusual event" or "unusual char-acter." The gauge for determining the length of the play this idea will engender is not *how* unusual it (or he/she) is, but rather how widespread the *ramifications* of the digression from the norm are.

Many unusual events or characters you come up with will feature some oddity or eccentricity that is of a completely natural origin, such as the fellow we mentioned earlier with several computers in each room of his house. Something like this does not, on the surface, appear to af-fect too many people and will be, consequently, better suited for the one-act format. If the unusual event or char-acter is of supernatural (or extraterrestrial) origin, on the other hand, such as the Uncle Charley/statuette scenario discussed earlier, or almost any idea involving UFO aliens, most likely a great many people will be affected, and we're usually talking three-act material here.

This is not to say that every full-length comedy has to have a supernatural or extraterrestrial element in it. There are a good many members of the species *Homo Sapiens* (as I am sure you are aware) who can have three-act eccentricities!

Characters

Another gauge you can use to determine in which format any given idea will work best is the number of characters who will be needed to fully explore the theme. Remember that full-length comedies usually are written for 25-30 characters. Most one-act plays feature ten or fewer roles. One-act plays written for holiday use (particularly Christmas) can include more characters than usual, especially if you include choral singing of popular Christmas carols as part of the play. Directors of Christmas plays generally have a larger pool of potential actors to draw upon. At Christmas time, it seems, everybody wants to get into the act.

Plan on incorporating more eccentrics than usual in your one-act plays. This is because it is much easier to establish an eccentric's identity in your audience's mind than it is to do likewise for a normal character. Normal characters require much more character development, and there is very little room for character de-velopment in the one-act format. Eccentrics, by their very nature, regularly do things that are, well...*eccentric*. In the space of a few well-crafted lines, a playwright can effectively let an audience know everything it needs to know about an eccentric character (and get a laugh or two in the bargain!).

The running gag works well in this format.

Laugh line set-ups constructed around the antics of an eccentric generally require less dialog than they would for a normal character. The audience already expects them to do things that are silly, so that's half the battle right there.

Use the same female/male (65%-35%) ratio as you would for a full-length play. The same proportion of girls and boys will turn out for play tryouts, regardless of the show's format.

The Plot

The plot structure of a one-act play should revolve around a single, sustained theme, as opposed to the architecture of three-act comedies, which allow room for sub-plots and other tangential plot elements. The time constraints of single-act plays quite simply do not permit adequate development of more than one theme. If a theme cannot be fully explored, there really is no reason to introduce it in the first place. Attempting to do so will only result in a great deal of audience frustration, which will be very detrimental to a play's popularity.

Strangely enough, the classic formula (get your hero up a tree, throw rocks at him, get him back down again) works as well in shorter plays as it does in their full-length counterparts. Of course, the trick is to accomplish all of this in under an hour. (Did I mention that writing one-act plays could be harder than producing longer scripts?)

Obviously, the injection of sub-plot elements into the play while trying to stick to this formula will result in the waste of valuable on-stage time and will inevitably serve no other purpose than to distract the audience. Many sub-plots in longer plays exist for the primary purpose of giving the second-string principals "something to do" in the show. There is no need for this in a one-acter because there are far fewer characters, and all of them should be involved one way or another with the central theme itself.

Dialog

Obviously, the "rules" for creation of dialog as explained in the chapter on "The Mechanics of Dialog" remain exactly the same as for a three-act play. Shorter plays still require the same compact, polished, easy-to-learn speeches that flow naturally and provide logical cues for subsequent lines as do longer scripts. In addition, the long monologues that are so problematic in a three-act play can be even more so in a shorter play. There is less time, which means fewer lines of dialog, to work with here.

I have already explained the importance of making each speech serve a specific purpose (exposition, moving the plot along, or humor). In a one-act play, where there is much less time to accomplish all these ends with your dialog, there are many places where a line must do "double duty," i.e., move the plot along *while* getting a good laugh. That's why it is so important to master the techniques of writing lines that effectively perform one of the three functions before attempting to apply such skills to the one-act format where, quite often, such "dual-purpose" lines are required.

In my one-act play, *Son Of "A Christmas Carol,"* I had set myself the task of writing a parody of the popular Dickensian tale. As I'm sure you are aware, there are a great many dramatized versions of *A Christmas Carol*. All are full-length productions, as there is simply no way to adequately present the story in a shorter format. So, here I was trying to squeeze a parody of all the important events of *A Christmas Carol* into my one-act comedy.

Early in my play, the audience finds out that the E. Scrooge in this play is not named after his great-grandfather, Ebenezer, but rather for his great, great grandfather, Englebert Scrooge. My Scrooge is even more crotchety than his ancestor. When the Ghost of Christmas Past comes for him, he refuses to go, much to the ghost's chagrin:

```
CHRISTMAS PAST: You can't refuse me; I'm the
                Ghost of Christmas Past!
       SCROOGE: I don't care if you're the
                Spirit of Saint Louis!
```

Two pages later, I have the Ghost of Christmas Present appearing on the scene. Since Scrooge has refused to go with Christmas Past, she is still there when her sister Ghost arrives. At this point, I needed to make the one ghost aware of the other's presence (advancing the plot) with as little dialog as possible. I managed to do this by combining this function with a laugh in the following two short lines:

```
CHRISTMAS PRESENT:  (Solemnly stepping toward
                    Scrooge and extending her hand.)
                    Ebenezer Scrooge IV, I presume.

CHRISTMAS PAST:     (Who had been unseen by
                    the other ghost until now.) It's
                    Englebert, dearie.
```

Comedy

All of the various types of jokes and laugh lines described in the chapter on comedy can be utilized in shorter plays in much the same manner as they are used in longer scripts; however, be aware that writing gags for one-act plays is a little trickier than for full-length comedies, as less on-stage time can be allocated to each joke. Set-up lines will have to be carefully honed and polished, with special attention paid to the elimination of unnecessary verbiage.

When writing comedy in the one-act format, playwrights need to get to that all-important first laugh of the show even sooner, and it should be, if possible, even more of a knee-slapper than it might be in a longer play. Things happen quickly here. With multi-purpose dialog, audiences are asked to absorb rapid-fire exposition and plot development *and* laugh while they are doing it! If you don't "hit them over the head" with a dynamite laugh line right off the bat, they may lose sight of the fact that they are watching a *comedy* somewhere in the shuffle.

One form of joke that works particularly well in this format is the running gag. There are two reasons for this. The first is that once established as such, a running gag (if not overused) brings *immediate* laughter from the audience. They already know this is a funny bit, so there is no hesitation on their part. And it is very important that the laughter be sustained throughout shorter plays, because once they stop laughing for any length of time, there might not be enough time left in the show to get them started again. The second is that a running gag provides a kind of cohesion to a short comedy. It's analogous to a belt or girdle encircling the play and drawn tightly so as to keep the various elements within together in the audience's mind.

When a running gag does double duty and also provides you with a curtain closing laugh, it can provide a neat little coda to your play. For example, in my one-act play *Murder Most Fowl*, I used a running gag that revolved around my Watson never being quite able to recall the technical names of various body parts. When the central action of the plot was effectively concluded, this is how I used that to bring my curtain down:

```
JONES:    {PRIVATE} Well, Watson, I guess
          I've wrapped this case up.

WATSON:   Hmmm.  Indeed.  I'm so happy for you,
          Jones. (Moving to chair, sits.) Now, if
          you don't mind, I really have to
          study. (Flips open book.) I think I
          have the bone structure of the
          foot down. How about quizzing me on
          the digestive system, Jones. You,
          er...don't seem to be otherwise occupied
          at the moment.

JONES:    (Sighs, moves to sofa, takes book
          from WATSON.) Very well, Watson. (Looks
          at book.) First question: Name the
          tubular passage running through the
          entire body for digestion and absorption.

WATSON:   Oh, yes. The something or other canal.
          It starts with an "A." Albatross or
          Algonquian or...
```

```
JONES: (Sighs)  Alimentary, my dear Watson.
       Alimentary.
```

CURTAIN

Miscellaneous One-act Topics

The two words that should govern your choices in any aspect of the creation of one-act plays are *less complex*. We have already seen how all the various elements of playwriting in this shorter format (idea, plot, characters, etc.) require a scaling down from what is needed for a full-length script. This carries over to the peripheral components of this medium as well.

Sets, for example, should be as simple as possible. I've already mentioned all the reasons why a single set is almost mandatory in a three-act play written for the amateur market. The reasons for a single set remain the same in the one-act format; however, that set should be as basic as possible. Quite often, more than one short play is used for an evening or afternoon's entertainment in the amateur field. It is very important that the set for any given play in the show be one that can be quickly struck[1] so that it can be cleared and the set for the next put into place and ready to go during the space of the normal twenty-minute intermission that is usually used between each individual one-acter in such a production. Complex sets with stairways, multi-level platforms, and heavy or large pieces of furniture would make such a quick change of scenery difficult, if not outright impossible.

The need for as simple a set as possible exists regardless of the intended use of a short play. Plays used in competitions will likely be presented along with several others in the same evening and so will have the same need for a set that can be quickly struck. If a play is going to be used as part of a larger program, it will quite likely have a

---

1. Theatre terminology for removal of scenery from the stage. To "strike the set" means to clear it from the stage.

very small budget for scenery, particularly if it is (as many are) a "one-night stand."

Lighting, sound, and costuming for one-act plays, likewise, need to be as simple as possible, for many of the same reasons as given above for scenery. Ideally, you should be only calling for "lights up" at the beginning of the play and "lights down" at the final curtain. A blackout to indicate passage of time should not present a problem. However, scripts should avoid complex lighting changes such as spotlights brought up to pinpoint a character or piece of scenery at some point in the play or the use of a follow-spot.[2]

Sound effects should be limited to simple things like phones or doorbells ringing. More complex sound effects that typically require a sound system should be avoided, because such a system may not be available where the play is to be performed, and installing one just for the play would probably be prohibitively bothersome (and expensive, if one must be rented!).

Likewise, groups will shy away from spending the money needed to rent period costumes for a short play, so you're much safer sticking to contemporary costuming as much as possible.

One thing that is virtually identical for either one-act or full-length plays is the manuscript format. In the next chapter we'll be taking a look at how to prepare the manuscript of your play for presentation to publishers in a professional manner .

---

2. A follow-spot is a powerful, long range spotlight typically operated from the back of a theater (behind the audience) and used to literally "follow" an actor as he or she moves around the stage.

Chapter Thirteen

Manuscript Format And Submission

It is said that you can't tell a book by its cover. While this may be true, a publisher can learn a lot of information about a playwright from the outward appearance of the manuscript he or she submits for consideration. This is a time when first impressions do count very much. An experienced publisher (and most of the publishers who specialize in plays for amateur use are quite experienced!) can take one quick glance at the contents of your large manilla envelope and decide right then and there whether he should spend the time evaluating your play or stuff it right back into the SASE[1] that accompanied it. So, you want to put your best foot forward when presenting you work. Here's how.

The Title Page

Your title page is the one place where you can afford to get a little fancy (but not too fancy!). Most word processors have

---

1. I'll assume that you already know that SASE is an acronym for Self-Addressed, Stamped Envelope. And you will include one with any submission of a play script that you make. Got that? Good. If you do not include a SASE, not only will the publisher not return your manuscript, the odds are he won't even read it! Publishers prefer to deal with professional writers, and professional writers *always* include SASEs.

the ability to let you select and scale your fonts. You can allow yourself the luxury of selecting a nice catchy font in a fairly large size (18-24 points) for the title of your play. Don't use a particularly garish font or one that is so highly stylized that it is difficult to read. Center your title at a spot around 1/3 of the way down the title page. Skip a line; then in a much smaller, italicized but not fancy font,[2] center the phrase: "A Comedy In Three Acts." Skip another line, drop the italics and center the word: "By." One more skipped line, and then you center your name or pseudonym.

Now, move to the lower right hand of your title sheet and in a normal typewriter font, such as Courier, put your name, address, Social Security number, and (optionally) E-mail address. For an example of what your title page should look like, see the sample on page 150.

Incidentally, the rest of your manuscript will be in this normal typewriter script, which is usually the default script of your word processor. Don't try to jazz things up by using a fancy font. Once again, this is a non-professional tactic, one that will instantly be picked up and looked askance at by a publisher.

In addition, everything you key in from this point on *must be double spaced.* If you've done any professional writing at all, you are already aware of this, but I mention this just in case writing a play is your first foray into the wonderful world of the wordsmith. Don't try to save paper by single spacing your pages. Likewise, don't attempt to snow the publisher into believing that your play is longer than it actually is (you won't, so don't bother trying) by triple spacing. Double spacing is the standard method of submitting any writing at all for publication. Anything else is unprofessional.

The Catalog Insert

The next pages in your manuscript will be used for what is called the *Catalog Insert.* This is exactly what it

---

2. I use Geneva Italicized, 14 point, but you can use any you prefer. Try for a "sans serif" type font, which is one without the little serif lines that shoot out from the tops of many letters.

One Heck Of A Play!

A Comedy In Three Acts
By
John Q. Playwright

John Q. Playwright
Broadway & 42nd Street
New York, NY 10036
SSN: 123 45 6789
Phone: 1-212-555-1212
FAX: 1-212-555-1234
Email: Plays@darngood.com

sounds like—copy that the publisher can utilize (she will probably edit it somewhat) for the page that will be used to promote your play in her catalog. You will essentially be giving a capsule summary of the salient points of your play. Don't be afraid to go a little "Madison Avenue" here. Be upbeat and enthusiastic. If you are not willing to promote your own work, why should the publisher?

Start with a snappy, attention-getting paragraph. Here's the opening of the catalog insert for my play *Go, Go, Go, UFO!*:

```
Shades of Star Wars!  The Venusians have
landed in New Jersey!  Has the invasion of
Earth begun?  Will the East Coast soon be
vaporized by phaser blasts?  Is it The War
Of The Worlds come true?
```

Follow this with a 250-300 word summary of the plot. Don't be boring with this. You are writing promotional material here, not a book review. End with a paragraph that includes a line or two of pure hype, something on the order of: "It's a laugh-a-minute in this gag-filled, hilarious comedy! The audience may have to take some time to stop laughing and compose themselves before leaving the theater!"

Skip a line and give the male/female (indicated, surprisingly enough, by the initials m and f) cast breakdown and set requirements in parenthesis thusly:

```
(10m., 15f., doubling possible. One interior set.)
```

I would suggest providing two catalog inserts, one long (as described above) and another shorter. Title both inserts accordingly. In the shorter version, keep the opening and closing paragraphs but cut the plot summary to under 100 words. The purpose of this is to accommodate the publisher's needs if he decides to devote less than a full page in his catalog to advertising your play. Don't be insulted, by the way, if your script doesn't rate top billing. Not every play merits a full page. You have come very far as a playwright if he decides to include your play in his catalog, regardless of the space it is given!

Providing catalog insert information, particularly in both long and short formats, adds a *very* professional touch to your presentation of your manuscript.

The Remaining Pre-Dialog Pages

After your catalog inserts, the next sheet will be a clear copy of your set diagram. Don't scrimp on paper; use a full sheet for this. You should put another copy of your set diagram, one that is done on heavy bright white paper with dark black ink (or toner) and is considered "camera-ready," in the folder that will accompany your submission. More about this folder later.

The next sheets will contain the following information: Cast of Characters, Time, Place, and Synopsis of Scenes (see page 153). Rather than describe how to present this information, it is easier to show you what typical sheets look like. The asterisk lines between sections are of my own devising. You can use something else to indicate breaks between them, if you like, on pages where more than one section fits comfortably.

Make outfitting the actors in the play as inexpensive as possible.

Follow with a list of properties, on-stage first (those props, including furnishings, that are on-stage when a curtain rises), and personal props (those that are carried on by an actor) next. The format for this is flexible. Here's an idea (much abbreviated) of the one I use (page 154).

Next will come your remarks on costuming for the play. Try to include anything that potential producers need to know about the costumes; however, remember to keep your costume requirements as flexible as possible. You should include any ideas you can think of that might make outfitting the actors in the play as inexpensive as possible. In addition,

CAST OF CHARACTERS
(In Order Of Appearance)

JOHN DOE

JANE DOE

BOB PARKER

UNCLE JOE

GRANDPA

****

TIME

The Present

PLACE

The living and dining room area of
the Does' home.

****

SYNOPSIS OF SCENES

ACT   ONE
Late one Friday afternoon in May

ACT   TWO
Immediately following

ACT   THREE
Scene 1: One week later
Scene 2: Several hours later

PROPERTIES

Onstage:

Armchair
Sofa
End table (2)
Coffee table
Bookcase filled with books and video cassettes
Television (console)
Telephone (on end table)
Telephone Directory
Vase with flowers (on coffee table)

Personal:

JOE: Attache case, newspaper, bag
of potato chips.
MARY: Tray with two cups of tea,
sugar bowl and creamer,
paperback novel,broom.
BOBBY: Comic book, toy truck, checker
board and checkers.
GRANDPA: Pipe and tobacco, deck of
cards.
MRS. JOHNSON: Purse, lipstick and nail polish
(inside purse).
FIRST POLICEMAN: Nightstick, book of summonses
SECOND POLICEMAN: Nightstick

you might pass along anything from your initial production that might prove helpful. You simply put all of this information in a normal paragraph format. Here's what appears in the published edition of my play *Off With His Head*:

COSTUMING

Costuming for *Off With His Head* is contemporary. Madame Bali's outfit is a bit more flamboyant than would ordinarily be seen on the street, and the sorcery caftans worn by Carol and Tony should be covered by brightly colored cabalistic symbols. (NOTE: One church production[3] found that cabalistic symbols cut out of brightly colored felt and sewn onto black choir robes worked very effectively.) Carol and Tabby should be close enough in size for them to wear the same clothes, as Tabby borrows a gown from Carol's wardrobe during the play.

Lighting and sound cues come next (don't worry, we'll get to the dialog soon!). They should be listed in chronological order and numbered sequentially. Divide them into groups (also listed sequentially) by act and scene. The effect itself should be in upper case letters and should be followed by the cue (the line that is spoken right before it). An example:

```
ACT ONE, Scene 1:
(1)  DOORBELL
Cue: MARIE: Did you think I'd forget my
             own name?
(2)  PHONE RINGS TWICE
Cue: BOBBY: I'm not going to just sit here
             all day.
```

3. This was my initial pre-publication production.

Finally, you should include a list of any production hints you might think of. This is another reason why you should follow your initial production closely. You can incorporate any tricks the director or technical director came up with to make the production run more smoothly (and cheaply!).

The Dialog

I told you we'd get to the dialog sooner or later! And now we're ready to record those brilliant lines you've created for your characters to say...almost. As I explained in Chapter Seven, we first have to put down the "Setting" and "At Rise" information for Act I, Scene 1. It is absolutely necessary to describe the setting of the scene and what is going on onstage as the curtain rises at the beginning of every scene. Since we have been concentrating on single-set shows, the "Setting" information for all of the following scenes will merely be: "Same as Act One, Scene 1." For the opening scene, though, we have to include the setting information just as described in Chapter Seven.

The format for this is simple. About 1/3 of the way down your first dialog page for the first act[4], center the title of your play using initial caps on the words (the first letter of each word is capitalized). Skip two lines and center the words: "ACT ONE" in upper case letters. On the next line, again center the words: "Scene 1." (Use the numeral rather than the word for the scene number here.) Skip a line or two, type the word "SETTING:" at the left margin. Hit the "Enter" key to move to the next line. Set the indent to ten spaces from the left margin. Type all the "Setting" information at this indented position. This will put your set description two spaces from the colon at the end of the word "SETTING." This is where you want to be. Use the indent command rather than just hitting the "Tab" key. This will automatically word-wrap all of the text for the description of your set to this tab setting.

When you have finished entering all the setting data,

---

4. The title of your play is only used at the beginning of Act One. The first page of dialog for Acts II and III does not use the play title, but other than that is formatted exactly the same.

skip a line and type the words: "AT RISE" at the left margin. Again, move to the next line, indent ten spaces, and describe exactly what is going on on-stage as the curtain rises as discussed in Chapter Seven.

Now you can begin entering the dialog. Before explaining the format for this, let me point out that this is the manuscript format. It differs from the format the play will be printed in. All of the excerpts from my plays reproduced within these pages were *not* in the manuscript format. They were in the printed format, which is easier to read. (The manuscript format, however, is easier to *edit*, and that's why it must be used.)

Stage directions go on their own line.

The character name is centered in upper case letters. On the next line, the spoken dialog is typed using normal left-justified text. Don't use full justification; left-justified text is easier to edit. Stage directions go on their own line, are indented three tab stop (fifteen spaces), and are bracketed. If, for example, a character's speech is three sentences long, and a stage direction occurs between the second and third sentences, you would type the first two sentences together. Then you would hit the Enter key, then the tab key three times, and insert the direction.[5] Finally, you would hit the carriage return again and key in the final sentence from the left justified position.

Skip a line, type in the name of the next character to speak in the same manner as the first, and take it from there. Character names are also typed in uppercase letters when they are part of a stage direction. When a name is spoken in dialog, it is merely initial-capped as it is in normal prose. Entrances and exits (the words "ENTERS" and "EXITS") are also keyed in in upper case.

Here's how the dialog about Emily, Mrs. Pincus, and

5. If the direction is longer than a few words, substitute the indent code your word processor uses for the third "tab," so that the entire stage direction wraps automatically to the correctly indented position.

the cup of sugar reproduced in Chapter Ten would look in manuscript format (as best as can be reproduced on this size of page):

<pre>
                        EMILY
         I'll get your sugar so you can leave.
                  (She turns and heads for the
                   kitchen doorway.)

                        MRS. PINCUS
         Wait a minute. You forgot the cup.

                        EMILY
                  (Pausing and turning back.)
         I don't need it, I'm
         going to give you the whole bag.

                        MRS. PINCUS
         But I only need a cup.

                        EMILY
         I know, but you can keep the bag anyway. That way,
         the next ten times you need to come over and borrow a
         cup of sugar from me, you can do it without coming
         over!
                  (She turns and EXITS.)
</pre>

Each scene ends with the word: "CURTAIN" in upper case letters centered on its own line. If you use a blackout to end a scene, center this in upper case letters on its own line also. If you use a blackout in the middle of a scene to indicate passage of time, use upper case letters for the entire statement, and put it in brackets on its own centered line:

<pre>
(THERE IS A BLACKOUT TO INDICATE PASSAGE OF TIME)
</pre>

The following two pages will give you an idea of how this looks all together in the proper manuscript format:

I-1-1

Burning Your Bridges!

ACT ONE
Scene 1

SETTING:

The waiting room of the dental office of
Dr. I. Yankem. There is a door in the Up
Left corner of the upstage wall. This
is the door to the office. Just to the
right of this door is the nurse's desk,
which is set a few feet away from the
upstage wall. There is an open appoint-
ment book on the desk and a few ordinary
desk tools (pencils, pens, scratch pad,
etc.) on the desk. A small chair for
the nurse is located directly behind the
desk. The door to the dentist's work
room is located along the right wall
about four feet from the upstage wall.
Chairs for waiting patients are located
along the rest of the right wall and the
entire left wall.

AT RISE:

        The NURSE is seated at her desk and is

        putting nail polish on her nails. Several

        patients are seated in the chairs along

        either wall. The door to the office opens

        and JOHN, a middle-aged man, ENTERS. He

        is holding his jaw as if he is in great

        pain. He moves to the desk and tries to

        get the NURSE's attention; however, she

        completely ignores him.

                    JOHN

Excuse me, Miss. I need to see the doctor right away.

                    NURSE
          (Without looking at him. She is
           completely absorbed in doing her nails.)

It's Ms.

                    JOHN

All right. Excuse me, *Ms.* I'm in a lot of pain.

                    NURSE
           (Still not looking at him.)

Take two aspirins and call the doctor in the morning.

Page numbering is a little more complicated than that of a normal manuscript. The preliminary information (catalog inserts, cast of characters, set design, sound and light cues, etc.) is generally not numbered at all. Individual publishers have their own preferences for placement of this material within printed copies of their plays. Some put it all up front. Others break it up, putting Cast of Characters, Time and Synopsis of Scenes up front and the rest in the back of the script. Numbering these pages serves no real purpose, and might even be confusing, once they are rearranged for publication.

The actual pages of dialog for the play have their own unique numbering system, which you may have noticed was used on the two sample pages just given. Act, scene, and page of the scene are indicated in the upper right hand corner of each page in the following format: An upper case Roman numeral for the Act number, a hyphen, a normal number for the scene number, a hyphen, and a normal number for the page of the scene. Act One, Scene 1, Page 1 looks like this: I-1-1

The page numbering begins again at "1" for each scene. For example, if Act One, Scene 1 has twenty-four pages, the last page of that scene would be numbered: I-1-24. The very next page, which would be the beginning of Act One, Scene 2, is numbered: I-2-1. *Always* start a new scene on its own page.

To Bind Or Not To Bind

If that's the question, the answer is bind, but not by any method that would make removal and rearranging of the pages a problem. If you've done any freelance article or short story work, you know that the pages for that particular type of submission are not stapled or bound at all, except for a paper clip at the top. Book-length manuscripts are usually submitted unbound inside typewriter paper boxes (which are getting harder to find, as most computer paper is sold in reams wrapped in paper!).

Play manuscripts are a unique case. They are not small enough to be held together with a paper clip, even a large-sized one. And unlike book-length manuscripts, which are generally too unwieldy to read comfortably if bound, plays fit nicely into report folders that are designed to hold a half-inch or so report. Of course, you would have to punch them for three-hole binding if you choose to use one. You can also buy reams of paper already punched for three-hole binding for your printer at any stationer. Your only task would be a little experimentation to see which way to load pre-punched paper into your printer to insure that it prints your pages with the holes where you want them to be.

I prefer the type of report cover that has two three-inch plates that lock the pages tightly by means of a little lever. This type of binder doesn't require the punching of holes into the pages of the manuscript. Unfortunately, these are getting harder to find at stationers, as they are not too popular in the business world. When I find a store that has some, I usually buy all they have.

Whichever method you choose, be sure to accompany your submission with an additional folder of the type that has a pocket on the inside of each cover. In this folder, you would use one pocket for a camera-ready copy of your set diagram and copies of any promotional material and reviews from your initial production or public reading, if you have one, and the other to hold two 3 1/2" floppy disks. On the first, include copies of the manuscript files in plain ASCII format. There is plenty of room on these disks, so you can devote an appropriately labeled separate file to each element of your preliminary material, as well as one for each scene of your play. If your word processor does not automatically put a ".TXT" extension on ASCII files, do it yourself. I label my dialog files this way:

    ACT1_SC1.TXT
    ACT1_SC2.TXT
    ACT2_SC1.TXT

...and so forth. I don't bother with using the Roman numeral convention here, because DOS gives you only eight characters to work with, and labeling the files for Acts Two and Three would naturally cause a problem. Your preliminary information can go into files labeled:

SET.TXT
CAST.TXT
LIGHTING.TXT
PROPS.TXT
...and so forth.

The second disk should carry identical information formatted for whichever word processor you are using. These files should have a different dot extension (not ".TXT"). Some word processors automatically add a distinctive dot extension. If yours does not, make up one or use ".DOC," a common extension for formatted word processor files. Just be sure that the extension you use is not ".EXE," ".COM," or ".BAT," as these extensions mean specific things to the computer. Use the exact same file identifiers to the left of the dot as on the ASCII version, so there is no confusion. Be sure to label each disk with your name, the name of the play, and the format of the files contained on it. On the disk with files formatted for your word processor, be sure to identify which word processor you have used along with its version number.

Label each pocket of this folder appropriately. Make sure that you do this because the disks slip down into the pocket (and out of sight) and may be unnoticed otherwise.

The Cover Letter

I always include a cover letter with my submissions. I suggest you do likewise. Keep the information in your cover letter to the essentials. Don't use it to explain why you feel your play would be perfect for the publisher. He or she can readily ascertain all of this by scanning your catalog insert (a good reason to spend some time on the preparation of same!). Basically, you want to indicate in your cover letter that you are submitting the enclosed manuscript for consideration for possible inclusion in their catalog of plays for amateurs. If you have a published history, you can mention this *briefly*, particularly if you have written on any theatre-related topics. Once you begin to have some of your plays in print, you can also mention this, again briefly.

Some publishers want to have a brief summary of the plot and nature of the play included in your cover letter.

Check "submission guidelines" sheets carefully, as many do not. If the publisher you are considering wants such a summary, be as brief as you can. You can mention that catalog inserts are included for a more detailed description of the story of the play.

Do state the fact that your play has been produced or has had a public reading and that you have included material related to this production or reading. Be sure to also indicate your willingness to revise the script, if necessary. I usually put this information in the sentence that mentions my inclusion of a SASE: "I have enclosed a SASE for return of the manuscript if you do not wish to use it or wish to return it for revision."

Above all, be polite and professional. Don't try to dazzle the publisher with your footwork in your cover letter, because you won't.

The Query Letter

As you check through the various listings in the markets chapter, you will see that some publishers prefer to see a query letter before an author submits the entire script for consideration. A query letter is a useful tool to publishers and playwrights alike. It gives the publisher an opportunity to quickly review the story and format of the play to see if it is consistent with the type of material she features in her catalog. She can accomplish all of this without having to plow through the complete script.

The playwright benefits in two ways. First, it saves him or her the trouble of carefully bundling up the manuscript and all the accompanying material and mailing same off to publishers for whom doing so would be waste of time, since the play is inconsistent with their current needs or format. By the use of query letters before submitting manuscripts, this effort would have to be made only for those publishers who expressed an interest in seeing the full script.

The second reason is an even greater time-saver for playwrights. Publishers almost always take two, three, or more months to review a manuscript; however, they respond to query letters in two weeks on the average. If you have selected a publisher who is not interested in your play, at least you won't have to wait 1/4 of a year to find this out!

A query letter should present the pertinent information about the play in the first paragraph (length of play, number of male and female characters, targeted audience, etc.). It should also contain information about the publishing history of the author, and any theatrical education or practical experience with the production of amateur plays he or she may have.

Use Priority Mail, or at least First-Class Mail.

Rather than include a summary of the play in the body of the letter, I prefer to include a copy of the long catalog insert (appropriately labeled as such). Doing this serves the dual purpose of telling the publisher what the story of the play is about and impressing her with your professionalism (by virtue of the fact that you *have* created a catalog insert).

Submitting Your Script To A Publisher

While it is fine to query several publishers at the same time, manuscripts should never be sent to more than one publisher at a time. This is different from the accepted norms for novel writers, who routinely submit their manuscripts simultaneously to several publishers. Writers of novels will send off copies of their manuscript to as many publishers as they can think of, or if they are wise, as many as indicate[6] they are open to unsolicited submissions of the genre they are writing in. The primary reason they do so is that they are competing in a market that is virtually flooded with unsolicited material; everybody seems to feel that they have at least one novel in them. Novel publishers, by necessity, can only devote so much time to manuscripts that come in over the transom. Often, an individual submission won't get looked at for months

---

6. Such listings are found in an accepted industry-wide standard reference such as *Writers' Digest Markets* or *The Writers' Handbook*.

after it arrives, and even then, a slush pile first reader will merely glance at the first page or two, and if not impressed, send it all back from whence it came.

Publishers of plays for amateur use generally devote more time to submissions. While many do have a long lead time (see the chapter on "Markets"), most will give your manuscript careful consideration when they do find time from their busy schedules to evaluate new work. Unless you've sent in a hastily written, unorganized, totally inappropriate script, your play will most likely be read through to the end. Quite often, those scripts that are rejected will be returned along with a nice, personal letter explaining why. If your play is not quite what they were looking for at the time, but they do like your writing, they will usually let you know that and may even encourage you to try them with your next script.

The market for amateur plays is not nearly as overwhelmed with unsolicited material as is that for novels. Far fewer people write plays than write prose fiction. Fewer still write *good* plays that are appropriate for the market. It is hoped that by following the guidelines presented in this book, you will become a part of that elite group.

Here's what should go into your envelope to the publisher: A fresh[7], loosely bound copy of the play and auxiliary material, the folder with the floppy disks, the camera-ready set diagram, and the promotional material and favorable reviews from your initial production, your cover letter, and a SASE. In addition, I find it useful to include a self-addressed postcard on which you have neatly typed: "The manuscript of your play (*name of your play*) has arrived at (name of Publisher)." The publisher will almost always return this card to you so you know that the play has arrived safely. On occasion, he will indicate on the card approximately how long you will have to wait for it to be evaluated.

Purchase some tough, expandable mailing envelopes

---

7. If your script is returned, do yourself a favor and print up a new copy to send to the next publisher. Paper and toner is cheap, and the computer's printer does all the work. You really don't want to give a publisher the impression that he or she was not your first choice by submitting an obviously used copy of the script.

to mail your submissions in and for use as your SASE's. I always put a piece of corrugated cardboard on either side of the package, within the envelope. This assures that any rough handling your package may receive in the mails won't affect the nice, professional-looking material you want the publisher to look at.

Once this is mailed off (use Priority Mail, or at least First-Class Mail; Book Rate, while undoubtedly cheaper, is chintzy and unprofessional), you've done your part. The next move is up to the publisher! While you're waiting to hear from him, why not begin work on your next play?

When The Answer Is Yes...

If your script is accepted for publication, you will, of course, be required to sign a contract. Unlike book contracts, which are long, complicated, and filled with pitfalls for the unwary first-novel writer, play contracts are short, to the point, and in clear English! Few run more than one side of a legal-sized sheet of paper. I would not waste money having a lawyer look them over. They are, for the most part, straightforward and clearly spell out your obligations and those of the publisher.

Your compensation will be either in the form of an outright purchase of amateur rights alone, outright purchase of all rights, or a royalty arrangement for either amateur rights only or all rights. Not many publishers, in my experience, seek to purchase all rights to your script.[8] Generally, they are concerned only with the rights to exclusively publish your play for amateur use and to lease your play for non-professional performance. With such an "amateur rights only" contract, you own all other rights. If a professional company (which usually means a group that is governed by Actor's Equity rules) wants to produce your play, or if someone wants to make a movie based on it, you alone control the rights to okay

---

8. If they do, and they are offering fair compensation, my suggestion is to sell. Very rarely do professional groups produce plays written for the amateur market. And I have yet to see a movie that started out as an amateur play. None of my many published plays has either had professional production or been made into a movie. I'm not complaining, mind you. That is simply the nature of the beast.

(and benefit from) such production.

If you are new to the field, you will most likely be offered an outright purchase contract. Several of my earlier plays were sold this way. Don't feel offended by such an offer. Play publishers, I have found, are quite fair. You simply have to "pay your dues" before moving up to royalty contracts. And you get paid up front in such an arrangement, always a plus for a struggling writer. You'll have to wait at least six months to receive any compensation at all from royalty contracts, as most publishers report sales to you and enclose their check for your share at six-month intervals.

Royalty contracts almost always offer 50% of all lease fees from amateur groups and 5-10% of playbook sales. If the latter seems a mite small, remember that most of a publisher's out-of-pocket expenses required to list your play in his catalog go into publication of the printed scripts. It is only fair that he receives a large percentage of the money from playbook sales. Most of it will simply be recouped expenses. If you doubt this, go to any printer and inquire how much it would cost to print up 500 or 1,000 copies of your script.

The nice thing about royalty arrangements is that money keeps on coming in, even if it is, after many years, only in drips and drabs. One of my plays (that I had written so long ago I would really have to read it again to tell you what it is about!) had, I thought, just about reached the end of its ability to earn money for me. Then, out of the blue, a group in California decided to produce an eighteen-performance run of it. My next royalty statement included a check for over $250. *Manna from Heaven!* I consider my royalty contracts as part of my old-age pension.

Chapter Fourteen

Revisions

Oy! I've Been Rejected!

First off, understand that a publisher's rejection of your manuscript is *not* a rejection of you or any reflection on your ability to write or to create a salable play. Rejection slips are a unfortunate fact of life, even for "established" writers. Novelists, authors of non-fiction books, magazine writers, journalists, yes, even playwrights are no stranger to those polite letters that start out: "Dear author, Thank you for your submission. Unfortunately, it does not meet our current needs..."

Even if the creation of a play in accordance with the excellent advice contained within the pages of this book is your first foray into the world of professional writing, I'm sure you are aware that not every piece submitted to a publisher is readily scooped up and rushed into print.

In fact, depending on the genre an author chooses to write in, the rejection rate by publishers can be anywhere from 75 to 99.9 percent of all submissions received, particularly when they arrive "over the transom," that is, unsolicited and unagented.[1]

1.Plays are, for the most part, not handled at all by literary agencies. This is not due to any disdain for theatrical pursuits on the part of agents. Agencies are geared to the selling of books (fiction and non-fiction). A play is an entirely different animal, one that requires significantly different methods of promotion and distribution. For the most part, you must learn to be your own publicist (this book will most certainly help you in that regard!).

Lest I frighten you and your manuscript away from the post office, let me assure you that a well-written play stands a much better chance of being read all the way through[2] and accepted for publication than literary works created in any other genre.

One of the nice things about being a playwright is that you will rarely receive that most dreaded of all communications that can show up in an author's mailbox: the form rejection letter. These impersonal, pre-printed rejections with little check-off boxes for the first readers[3] to tick off in order to tell you in broad, general terms why your manuscript has been returned to you are the bane of writers all over the world. It is very depressing to have spent months or even years producing a manuscript only to have it dismissed by a tick in a check-off box.

Play publishers, I am pleased to report, are for the most part much more considerate of authors who submit work to them. They like to encourage promising playwrights, and if they cannot use your play, they will usually take the time to send you a personal (not pre-printed) letter to tell you exactly why your play is not right for their catalog.

Sometimes the reason given is one which does not inspire you to revise the script and try that publisher again with it. If the rejection letter tells you that your play does not fit into any of the categories they list in their catalog, you would do well to try a different publisher, rather than consider a revision. For example, your play might have a science fiction theme (or a western theme, or a romance theme, or a religious theme, etc.) and they either do not publish those types of plays at all or have not had much success leasing those

---

2.This is an important consideration when you realize that most unsolicited novel manuscripts, even though they may have taken authors years to write, are often tucked neatly back into their SASEs and sent on their way after having no more than the opening paragraph of Chapter One read.

3.A first reader is one of those rare individuals whose job title completely describes the work he or she actually does. First readers open up all incoming unsolicited submissions and are the first (and most often the only) people to read them. Anything that they feel might possibly have the potential to meet the publisher's current needs will get passed up the ladder to an editor. The rest get promptly returned to the authors without anybody else in the company ever seeing them.

that they have published in the past.

This does not mean, however, that a different publisher might not have better success. Some publishers may very well have a special section in their catalog for just your type of play. Individual play producers have differing goals and requirements for their productions. They know exactly what type of play they are looking for and will select from catalogs that feature it, rather than from those that do not.

In the world of amateur theatre, one size most assuredly does not fit all. Play publishers tend to specialize (read the markets chapter carefully!). From a publisher's point of view, an attempt to please every producer who might peruse his catalog might cause a publisher to over-diversify, a fatal error considering the high cost of printing and publishing each individual play in his catalog. So, your script might be terrific but outside the categories a particular publisher is geared for, hence it is rejected by him.

When a Rejection Letter Is Not the Final Word from a Publisher

Quite often, the rejection letter you receive will imply (or even come right out and say) that the publisher might be willing to have another look at your play if it should be revised along this or that guideline. This is no guarantee that they will buy it if you do revise the script, even if you do so exactly the way the editor has suggested. But it is a strong indication that he does see things he likes in your play and is willing to work with you toward your ultimate goal of having your script included in his catalog of plays.

So, when this happens, what do you do? Some writers' first reaction may be one of horror.[4] "Revise *my* play, my *magnum opus?* How dare they suggest such a thing!" This is fine if you are content to leave your play unrevised, unproduced, and unpublished in its little folder in your file cabinet. This book, however, is about getting your play into print, so let's consider those revisions, shall we?

4.I know many (including playwrights) who feel this way about their work. None is published.

Let me precede my discussion of revisions by advising you to always—*always*—start by making a copy of the computer files for your play and work with these copies, rather than the original files, for your revision. That way, if your revision bogs down or if you are totally unhappy with it, you can always erase the working copies of the *revised* files, make a new set from the originals, and "go back to square one" for another try at a revision. Also, if the publisher for whom you are making the revision ultimately rejects the script anyway, you can try out your play in its original form with another publisher by printing up a fresh copy from your master (unrevised) copies of the files.

Types of Requested Revisions

In this chapter I'm going to address the most common suggestions publishers make for the revision of a script. Once you know how to handle them, you will be able to tackle any other sort of revision to your play in a professional manner.

Length

The *length* of a play is probably the *most frequent* problem publishers will find with a script. Your play might be too long, or even too short, for their needs. As I have mentioned above, different publishers seek to fill the needs of specific categories of amateur productions. For example, your play might take more than the usual two to two-and-a-half hours to perform. The publisher knows that the majority of potential producers who look through his catalog will shy away from scripts with long playing times. Another possibility is that your script might take significantly less time than usual to perform. It may be in that gray area: too long to be a one-acter, too short to provide a full evening's entertainment.

If your play is too short, there are a number of quick and easy fixes. First off, you could expand the role of one or more of the minor characters. A bit part might be expanded so as to give the player a little more stage time. If he or she is an eccentric, perhaps you might find a few more jokes to give that actor. Likewise a minor part or even a major part could be expanded to show a few more dimensions of the character. You might even consider adding a minor role.

I would *avoid* trying to add another principal character, though. Principal characters are generally those who impact on the plot. You risk upsetting the balance of the play if you attempt to add more elements to the plot. Moreover, principal characters are expected to impact the plot, and if you attempt to add a principal who doesn't impact on the plot, the natural question will arise among those producers who are considering your script: what is this character's function in the play? The answer is, of course, he is there just to make the play run longer. Not the kind of thing that adds to the desirability of your play.

It goes without saying that you should not try to lengthen the playing time by adding words (particularly adjectives!) to existing speeches. Recall that we spent time learning how to pare those unnecessary words from your dialog....

Cutting your script is a little trickier. The *easiest* way is to look for one or more bit parts or minor characters to trim or even eliminate from your script. Be sure, though, that nothing they do impacts on any other part of the play. If, for example, a character is responsible for bringing a needed prop on-stage and there is no believable way that that prop could be introduced into the play just by being on-stage already "at rise," you could trim that part but not eliminate it. Find a faster (fewer lines) way to have that character do his or her job and then exit. Or see if another character can believably bring the prop on-stage.

If the sole purpose for having a bit part is to have that character say a particular line that is important to the plot, perhaps you can find a way to assign it to another character.

A task that is harder, but may be just the trick if your play is running more than ten or fifteen minutes too long, is to see if one of your subplots can be eliminated. Cutting out a subplot has to be done with the skill of a surgeon because the entire play must be read over carefully to eliminate all references to that subplot. Also, chances are that doing so will make you lose some good laugh lines. Remember, though, that you can always use those lines, or even that entire sub-plot, in your next play!

With any cutting of your script, you should be particularly mindful of running gags. There are times that more than one character is involved with the running gag. If, for example, your running gag is used three times, and one of those times is by a character you are eliminating, you will have to see if another character can keep the running gag going for you.

Aspects of Your Character(s)

Another problem publishers can find with your script may center on an aspect of one of your characters. This will usually be one of your eccentrics. The characteristics of your eccentrics will, by definition, be odd to one degree or another. There are certain kinds of oddities that one publisher or another might be uncomfortable with, or just not see the humor in.

In one of my plays I had a character who was an avid comic-book collector, so much so that her entire life revolved around comic books. The publisher I submitted it to just did not care for the comic book motif. I realized right away that eliminating this aspect of the character would mean a major re-write of the entire play, but I thought I would give it a whack anyway. As things turned out, the eccentric aspect I replaced it with not only made the script a better play, but also ended up causing a significant alteration of the central plot. Further, it resulted in a name change for the play! The comic books were gone, but the new, improved eccentric character turned out to be a heavy metal music freak.

Incidentally, the publisher did not like this aspect of my character either, but another did, and so for my efforts, I wound up with a much improved play which is listed in the publisher's catalog under the title *Heavy Metal*.

Scenes and Subplots

There are also times when a certain scene or sub-plot does not sit well with a publisher. Without fail, it will be one of your favorites, but as has been already mentioned, it can always make its way into another play (but don't send that play to the same publisher!).

We've already covered the ways to excise subplots from a script in the case of a play that is too long, but remember that in plays that are of the right length, you will have to think up something to replace the stage time used by the material you are removing. In addition, anything important to the plot that occurs in that scene or within the framework of that subplot will have to find its way into the remaining scenes of your play.

If, in the original creation of your script, you added a scene "just for laughs," that is, just as an opportunity to add some additional humor to the play, and the scene does nothing to advance the plot (or even interrupts the flow of the play), a publisher will spot that right away. Of course, in such a case, the scene should be able to be cut without too much reworking of the remaining script, because the scene was superfluous to begin with.

Don't use dialect in your dialog!

Dialog Problems

If the publisher comments that your dialog does not seem "crisp," you should have another look at the chapter on dialog. More than likely, there are words (adjectives!) that you can still prune from your speeches without affecting the context of those speeches. A play will always benefit from "tighter" dialog. This is one time, by the way, that you should always consider making the requested revision. Play publishers are professionals, and they have seen many, many scripts. Chances are, if one publisher finds your dialog to be wordy, every other one also will.

You may also find that a publisher does not like your use of dialect for one or more characters. Few do, and for several good reasons. First of all, the creation of *good* dialect is an extremely difficult task, even for accomplished playwrights. In addition, dialect makes reading the play that much harder for the people who must decide whether or not to produce it. If they don't "get" the dialect, they will merely pass your script by in favor of one that does not force them to wrestle with dialect. So, let me repeat my earlier admonition: *Don't use dialect in your dialog!* If you feel that you absolutely must use dialect, it would do you well to examine the reasons for that decision.

Regardless of which revisions you choose to make to your play, you must always keep in mind that any alteration can (and most likely will) affect some or all of the peripheral material for your play. Property lists, lighting and sound cues, scene and cast listing, etc. must be scrupulously checked to make sure that they reflect the changes you have made.

Chapter Fifteen

A Few Final Words

W ell, now you are ready to add your contributions to the wonderful world of amateur theatre. And what an exciting place that is!

I have been involved with the thrilling and magical universe that is the amateur stage for over thirty years. In that time, I have been involved in more shows than I can enumerate. Even if I sat down and made a concerted effort to figure out exactly how many different productions I have been a part of in one way or the other, I would undoubtedly miss one or two here and there. Several of these productions were of my own work; however, it has been my distinct privilege to have acted in, directed, produced, worked sound and light boards for, designed and built scenery for, and been stage manager for many of the plays and musicals that have become part of American and World theatrical history, as well as shows that not many people have ever heard of, but have still managed to consistently entertain every audience they have ever been performed before. All of these productions I have participated in were on the stage of various amateur groups, both school and community theatre.

Ninety-nine percent of the media coverage of the theatre is centered around professional productions, on and off

Broadway and on the big screens of movie theaters and smaller screens of television. It has always been my contention, though, that if you want to see what is *really* going on in theatre, you have be part of the amateur scene, either as a participant or as a member of the audience. That's where you'll find the people who are truly dedicated to preserving the theatrical heritage for generations to come. Never feel that you are writing for "second string" theatre when you create plays for these fine people to perform. When you write for the amateur theatre, you are always on the "A Team," and don't forget it.

Most actors and other people associated with theatre hope to "make it" some day, and command the seven and eight figure salaries of the so-called "stars." Trust me, the first time you hear the sound of people laughing at jokes you have written into one of your plays, you will have the same exhilarating feeling of having "made it" as I have whenever the lights go down and the curtain rises on a show that I am proud to be a part of. And I wouldn't trade that for anything in the world (although I must admit that a seven figure salary would be tempting!)

So, what are you waiting for? Start tapping those keys and join in on the fun. The delightful world of amateur theatre anxiously awaits your first entrance (stage right).

I would enjoy hearing about your reactions to this book and about your experiences writing for the amateur stage. I can be reached by writing to the publisher or, if you are connected to cyberspace (and if you're not, why aren't you?) at one of the following E-mail addresses:

FrankVP@aol.com
75210.675@compuserve.com

One caveat, though. I will be glad to answer any of your questions about writing for the amateur theatre; however, do not send me scripts to review, comment on, etc. I do earn some small fees as a "play doctor" from time to time, and it would not be fair to people who have paid me for my work on their scripts to do so for others without charging a fee. If you would like to engage my services at my standard rates, fine. But write to me first and enquire. *Do not send scripts to me without receiving my okay.*

Once again, good luck and good writing to you. As for myself, I'm going back to work on the play I was in the middle of when I got the call to write this book. So, hold my calls; my characters and I will be in conference.

Frank V. Priore
College Point, NY
August, 1996

Glossary

Act Curtain: The main curtain of a stage, located just inside the proscenium. It is raised (or pulled side to side) to signal the opening of each act of a play, and lowered or closed to signal the end of each act of a play.

Apron: An area of the stage forward of the proscenium. It may be rectangular or curved.

Aside: A type of joke that requires the actor to direct a remark to the audience, rather than to another actor onstage.

Broadway: A play that is "On Broadway" is a professional production in one of the theatres in New York City which are designated as "Broadway Theatres." Most of the theatres are concentrated on Broadway itself, in the streets to the left and right of Broadway from approximately 41st Street to 57th Street, and the theatres that are a part of Lincoln Center for the Performing Arts in New York City.

Community Theatre: Non-professional and semi-professional theatrical troupes that perform in local communities around the country. Most Community Theatre groups include actors and directors with some professional credits, as well as many strictly amateur actors. All who are working and performing in Community Theatre productions are doing so for the love of the theatre, rather than for profit. (Also known as Regional Theatre and Little Theatre.)

Cyclorama: A large semi-circular drop that usually covers the entire upstage wall of a set.

Doubling: Using a single actor to perform two or more roles in a play. A very useful tool when cast size of a play is larger than available actors to perform in it. Doubling is usually confined to minor roles.

Downstage: The half of the stage closest to the audience.

Drawing Room Comedy: A type of farce, popularized by the British, which typically takes place entirely within the confines of a drawing room (a room for receiving or entertaining guests).

Drop: A curtain, usually of canvas or muslin, upon which a scene is painted.

Farce: Very light, humorous theatrical subject matter that has very improbable plot elements and uses characters that are usually larger than life.

Flat: Scenery wall section, typically four foot by eight, composed of canvas or muslin stretched over wooden frames, upon which set elements are painted.

Fourth Wall: An "invisible" wall that is the line of demarcation between the set and the audience. It is so named because most interior sets consist of three walls of a room. The "fourth wall," if it actually existed, would complete the box of the room (and would also completely block the set from the audience's view). Actors must be aware of the existence of this "wall," so that they do not "walk through it" while onstage. Many actors create this wall, and all its furnishings, in their minds to help them perform believably.

Little Theatre: See "Community Theatre."

Off-Broadway: Professional productions in New York City that are governed by many of the same rules as "On Broadway" shows; however, are not performed in one of the theatres designated as a "Broadway" house.

Off-Off-Broadway: Professional or semi-professional shows produced in New York City, but not in "Broadway" or Off-Broadway" theatres.

One-Liner: A joke that generally requires only one set-up line from a "straight-man" character.

Property: Or "prop." Any object, other than scenery, that is in place onstage or is carried onstage by an actor during the performance of a play.

Proscenium: An arch or frame that separates the stage from the audience.

Public Reading: A reading (as opposed to a performance) of a play in manuscript form by actors in front of an audience.

Query Letter: An inquiry to a publisher concerning a play an author has written. The letter explains the nature of the play, the number of characters, etc., and briefly summarizes the plot. The purpose of such a letter is to determine whether or not the publisher is interested in seeing the full manuscript of the play.

Regional Theatre: See "Community Theatre"

Running Gag: A series of jokes with a recognizable pattern of repetition in the form, words, or cadence of the jokes.

Set: An inclusive term for the scenery, furnishings, and properties that occupy the onstage playing area of a play. It represents the location wherein the action of the play occurs.

Sight Gag: A joke that is visual rather than a part of the dialog.

Stage (Set) Diagram: A schematic representation of the walls, doorways, windows and furnishings of a set.

Stage Left: The half of the stage that is to the left of an actor when he is standing on the stage and is facing the audience.

Stage Right: The half of the stage that is to the right of an actor when he is standing on the stage and is facing the audience.

Striking: Removal from the stage. To "strike the set" is to remove it from the stage.

Upstage: The half of the stage farthest from the audience.

Upstaging: The intentional movement of an actor into a position far upstage of another actor whose dialog requires him to speak to that actor. In order to deliver the lines to the upstage actor, the downstage actor would be forced to turn his head away from the audience, an undesirable situation. Intentional upstaging is considered extremely unprofessional.

Wing: A scenery section that is set up on either the extreme left or right side of the stage and extends into the offstage area. It serves as an entrance to the stage when actors move onstage from behind it.

Appendix

From The Files Of Frank V. Priore...

Throughout this book, I have been creating fictitious examples of the various elements of play creation (ideas, character sheets, dialog format, etc.). I think it would be helpful to your career as a budding playwright to see some actual examples from the files of my own published work, works in progress, and backlog of ideas and characters to be used in the future.

Ideas

Reaching down deeply into my "Idea File," I have come up with the tidbits below. I want to give you an example of the types of things that go into an idea file and may (or may not!) someday come to fruition as the basis of a play. All are copied verbatim from scraps of paper tucked into my file.

The first is just a few sentences that at some time in the future may form the basis of a plot or sub-plot for a play:

"Teenage girl comes to big city to live with older sister. She finds she has a crush on the mailman, so spends her days cutting out coupons from magazines and sending in for stuff so mailman will make lots of visits to house to deliver packages."

The second goes into a little more detail for an idea, and even contains a possible line of dialog:

"A Fat Vampire - (Fatula?). Resides in America, where so many people are overweight - lots of cholesterol in their blood. 'There's so much cholesterol in the blood I drink. If I wasn't dead already, I'd worry about getting a heart attack.' He can't change into a bat and fly away. When he does change into a bat, it is so fat it can't fly."

The last is just a joke dialog sequence without an accompanying plot idea:

"A: I'm going off in search of a lawyer.
B: Ah, just like Diogenes.
A: No. He was searching for an honest man. I'm looking for a lawyer."

Characters

Building A Character Library

Not every character created for a play actually gets used in that play. As the plot develops, you may find that one or more characters you have generated just won't work in the context of the show or are, in fact, unnecessary for this particular play. Don't discard the character sheets you have made for these individuals. They are valuable to you!

Sometime in the future, you might be able to use them in another play. One of them might actually spark an idea for the creation of a play built around that very character.

In addition, there are times when you may observe some unusual person in your travels (that is, something about him or her gets your attention). Why not create a character sheet based on what you've observed? You can fill in (create) the rest of that character's profile on your own, and voila! you have another character in your "library". Chances are, you won't have an immediate use for that character, but somewhere down the line, you undoubtedly will. Never let a creative opportunity pass you by. If you neglect to "capture" that character on paper right away, your memory of him or her will quickly fade.

Sort your "library" into normals, eccentrics, male, female, etc. Leaf through them when inspiration seems to fail you. Mix and match them, and think about what type of situation might bring one character together with another. Thus are plots built!

The following is a character sheet from my own "library" of characters. As you can see, it is a character that I want to someday base a play around.

CHARACTER SHEET

NAME: Benjamin Perkins AKA: Grandpa Benjy
TYPE OF CHARACTER: NORMAL [X]ECCENTRIC
GENDER: M AGE: 70
EDUCATION: Ph.D. in English Grammar
PREVIOUS OCCUPATION(S): High School English
Teacher (All his Working life)

ANY SIGNIFICANT HEALTH PROBLEMS: (None)
WHERE BORN: Boston
WHERE DID S(HE) GROW UP: Boston
WHERE ELSE HAS S(HE) LIVED: (Local, rural town
where play is set)
WHERE DOES S(HE) CURRENTLY LIVE: With daughter
and family
HOW LONG: Since retirement from teaching

SIGNIFICANT EVENTS IN CHARACTER'S LIFE:

MILITARY: (None)

MARRIAGE(S): One - Now widower

OTHER:

CURRENTLY MARRIED: YES [X]NO TO WHOM:____

WHAT DOES S(HE) DO TO RELAX: Always working on "his book." (Nobody has ever seen this book).

THINGS HE LIKES: Reading WHY: (He is educated) Playing Checkers WHY: He has never been beaten (and he plays: if you get one king you win, but he has to wipe you out to win!)

THINGS S(HE)
DISLIKES: Television, Movies WHY: "Warps your brain!"

(FOR NORMALS)
WHAT IS IT THAT MAKES HIM/HER SPECIAL:_____
_____

(FOR ECCENTRICS)
PRIMARY TRAIT: Constantly corrects everybody's grammar (to the point of extreme annoyance)
SECONDARY TRAITS (IF NECESSARY): Typical cranky old man
NOTES: Possible basis for a play: His daughter and husband are in dire need of money (primary "problem of play"). In Third Act this is solved by him, as he finally has "his book" published and it is an instant best seller. To everyone's surprise, it is not a scholarly work, but a trashy novel. (Why?) "How many books on English grammar make it to the best seller list!"

Setting

The following is the "Setting" information from my one-act play *Murder Most Fowl!*:

SETTING:

A large, somewhat dingy one-room apartment somewhere in the heart of a big city. Shabby furnishings abound, as well as several large cardboard boxes. The walls are lined with built in bookcases; however, there are very few books on them. Rather, shelf space is taken up by such unsavory items as half-filled soda bottles, empty cereal boxes, crinkled up potato chip bags, etc. There is a small sofa and armchair downstage left and a hutch downstage along the right wall. An end table next to the armchair has a phone on it. A large window with a ripped shade is along the backstage wall left of center. Through the window can be seen several old buildings across the street. There is a door right.

At Rise

Here is the "At Rise" text from another new play I am currently working on (I've also included the first line of dialog to show how the "At Rise" text leads directly into the dialog). As you can see, this is a "discovery" type of opening.

AT RISE:

> DORA, a lady in her mid-sixties sits in the downstage upholstered chair. She is avidly working on a crossword puzzle in a magazine. She is absorbed in her work and appears not to be interested in anything else going on around her, BOB, a fairly handsome man in his mid-thirties, is behind the front desk. He has one elbow on the desk and is resting his head on his hand. With his free hand, he is absently paging through a magazine on the desk. ANNIE, a lady in her mid to late forties, is seated at the table in the chair closest to the left wall. PATTY, a young girl in a maid's outfit, ENTERS from the kitchen. She carries a feather duster and quickly moves to the fireplace where she busily and vigorously dusts everything on or near the fireplace (the knickknacks, andirons, etc.,) with a feather duster. She quickly moves to the front desk. and begins dusting it. When she reaches BOB's elbow, he lifts it to the side (keeping his head on the hand and not looking directly at her) to let her dust under it, then replaces his elbow as she moves on. She then quickly

              moves to the table, dusts all around
              the objects, then moves to the large
              portrait of Catherine The Great on
              the left wall. She seems intent on
              removing every last mote of dust
              from the painting. This catches
              ANNIE's eye.

                            ANNIE
              Er, Patty. I think that painting
              has been dusted enough. Catherine
              the Great looks...just great.

And Now To Put It All Together...

    What better way to end a book on playwriting for the amateur market than to present the complete text of a play written for this market for your perusal? Below is the complete text of one of my (as yet) unpublished plays. It is in the category of a "short-short" play; i.e., it is much shorter than a standard one-act play. It is going into an anthology of skit-length plays I am working on. It is in standard manuscript format.

    After reading this play, you may wonder why I have called for such a lavish set for an amateur play. Remember that economy and ease of construction are important in this market. As I explain in the "Hints" (not reproduced here) for this play, most of the set can be painted on flats. Also, since only a few books are actually moved by the actors, most of the books in elegant bindings called for can also be painted onto the scenery flats.

    (Performance rights [amateur and professional] for *The Berican Collection Caper* are strictly reserved. Contact the author for information on performance rights.)

THE BERICAN COLLECTION CAPER
ACT ONE
Scene 1

SETTING:

> The library of the mansion of Mr. and Mrs.
> James Clarkton, wealthy socialites. It is a
> lavishly decorated room. Bookcases filled
> with leather-bound books line the walls.
> There are expensive chairs with small end-
> tables next to them in the down left and up
> right areas. The upstage wall features a
> window just right of center, a closet door
> just left of center and a portrait of Mr.
> Clarkton between them. The bottom of an
> elegant stairway opens into the extreme left
> corner. The stairway curves behind the
> upstage wall, and rises out of the
> audience's sight four or five steps up.

AT RISE:

        It is nighttime. The room lights are out,
but there is enough light in the room to
clearly see anyone onstage. There is sufficient darkness, however, for the beams of
bright flashlights to be distinguished from
the ambient light. No one is on stage.
After a few beats, the window opens slowly.
It is being opened by BOOMER, a burglar.
Before climbing through the window, he
shines a flashlight into the room. He EN-
TERS through the window, and lifts a satchel
filled with burglary tools in behind him.

BOOMER

(Snickering) I love breaking into rich guys' houses.
They have all kinds of locks on the doors, but they
always leave the windows open. Well, better get to
work. That Berican Collection must be around here
somewhere.

        (He shines the flashlight up and down on
        the walls. He moves to a bookcase left
        and removes some books, placing them
        gently on a chair. He feels around
        in the empty space on the shelf, then
        removes some more books.)

Now, where is that safe?

(As he continues removing books and
searching, another flashlight is seen
shining through the open window.
BOOMER, whose back is to the window,
does not see this. MUGGSY, another
burglar, ENTERS, climbing in through
the window. He shines his flashlight
on the right wall, moves to a bookcase
along that wall and removes books and
searches the back of the shelf just as
BOOMER is doing. Both work quietly and
are unaware of each other's presence.
A third flashlight appears in the open
window, and FINGERS, yet another burglar, ENTERS through the window, unseen
by the other two. FINGERS shines his
flashlight on the "fourth wall" (the
audience). Just then, both MUGGSY and
BOOMER stop, turn downstage, scratch
there heads in thought, then start
looking elsewhere. As they do the
three flashlight beams converge and the
burglars discover each other's presence.)

                    BOOMER
What the...?
          (Picking up MUGGSY's face in his beam)
Muggsy, that you?

                    MUGGSY
        (Shining his flashlight on BOOMER's face)
Yeah. What are you doing here, Boomer?

                    FINGERS
What are *both* of you guys doing here?
            (BOOMER and MUGGSY shine their flash-
            lights toward the sound of FINGERS'
            voice.)

            MUGGSY & BOOMER (Together)
Fingers!
            (All three move downstage, which has
            more light than the upstage area.)

                    FINGERS
What is this—a burglars' convention or something?

                    MUGGSY
(Trying to be casual) Heh, heh. What a coincidence.
All three of us pick the same house to hit.

                    BOOMER
(Also trying to be casual) Yeah, what a coincidence.
            (MUGGSY and BOOMER shuffle their
            feet a bit.)

FINGERS

(To the point) All right, let's cut out the baloney.
You two guys are here because of this, right.
                    (He pulls an article cut from a newspaper
                    from his pocket and shows it to them. As
                    if in acknowledgment, MUGGSY and BOOMER
                    pull identical copies of the article
                    from their pockets.)
Okay, then. The three of us read this morning's
newspaper. And were all here trying to heist this
"Berican Collection" they talk about in this article.

MUGGSY

That's about the size of it, Fingers.

BOOMER

So what do we do - flip to see who gets to stay and
pull the job?

MUGGSY

I don't like that idea. This Berican Collection must
be worth a lot. I mean, they wrote about it in the
papers and all. I want a piece of the action.

FINGERS

If this collection is worth as much as I think it is,
there's going to be plenty of loot to go around. We
can split it. And with three of us looking, we can
find it a lot faster.

                         BOOMER
Good thinking! What are we standing around here for?
Let's get to work.
              (They start to move away from
              each other.)

                        MUGGSY
Hey, any of you guys know just what kind of collection this is supposed to be? The newspaper doesn't
say.

                        FINGERS
It's got to be jewels. They don't give fancy names
like "The Berican Collection" to some sap's cigar
band collection. Wise up!

                        MUGGSY
Yeah, that's what I figured.

                         BOOMER
I'm sure it's jewels, and jewels are kept in safes.
I've been looking for a safe ever since I got here.

                        FINGERS
What's to look for? These rich guys are very predictable. All you got to do is...
              (He moves to the large portrait on the
              upstage wall)

FINGERS (Cont.)
...look for the biggest painting hanging on the wall.
It's always behind that.
            (He pulls it away from the wall. The
            picture is hinged on the right side, and
            opens like a door. A wall safe is
            seen behind the picture.)
What did I tell you?
            (BOOMER moves to the satchel of tools,
            and rummages around in it.)

                    MUGGSY
All right! Gee, you sure are smart, Fingers!

                    BOOMER
            (Moves to the safe. He has a glob of
            plastic explosive in his hands.)
Okay, guys. Stand back; I'm going to blow the safe.

                    FINGERS
            (Angrily takes the plastic explosive from
            BOOMER and tosses it aside.)
Give me that, you idiot. You want to wake up the
whole neighborhood or something?

                    BOOMER
But how are we going to get into that thing if I
don't blow it?

                    FINGERS
            (Makes an elaborate show of cracking the
            knuckles on both hands.)
They don't call me Fingers for nothing.
                    (Wiggles his fingers.)
I'll have this safe opened in thirty seconds flat.
            (He goes to work on the safe. As he
            does, another flashlight beam shines
            through the window. MUGGSY spots it.)

                    MUGGSY
Oh, no! Someone else is here! Don't tell me we're
going to have to split this loot *four* ways!
            (1ST POLICEMAN appears in the window.
            His other hand holds a drawn gun.)

1ST POLICEMAN
(Speaks with a heavy Irish accent) I don't think so,
lads.
            (He ENTERS through window, keeping the
            gun on them as he does.)
Let's put those hands up nice and slowly now.
            (They comply. 1ST POLICEMAN, keeping
            them covered all the while, moves to
            the door, opens it and lets in
            2ND POLICEMAN, who is carrying
            a billy club.)

2ND POLICEMAN

(Also speaking with an Irish accent) Well, what have
we got here - three naughty boys caught with their
fingers in the pie.

FINGERS

Ah, beans to you, copper!

1ST POLICEMAN

Now, now. Mind your manners, lad. I don't believe
in police brutality myself, mind you, but I'm afraid
he does.
            (He indicates 2ND POLICEMAN, who is
            smiling and slowly slamming his billy
            club into the palm of his other hand.)

MUGGSY

What rotten luck! The cops have got to be checking
out this house just on the night we hit it.

1ST POLICEMAN

There was no luck involved at all. You three were
shining flashlight beams back and forth like it was
an opening night in Hollywood. We spotted that two
blocks away. Besides, we've been keeping an eye on
this particular house all night.
            (He takes a copy of the same newspaper
            article out of his pocket.)
This look familiar, boys?
            (The burglars groan)

1st POLICEMAN (Cont.)

Yes, policemen read the newspapers, too, I'm afraid.
Whatever this Berican Collection is, we figured this
mention of it in the papers would probably bring all
you punks out of the woodwork to have a go at it.

2ND POLICEMAN

And it looks like we were right.
> (A door is heard opening and slamming
> offstage at the head of the stairs.
> The attention of all is drawn to the
> stairs, as suddenly the lights of
> the room come on, and PARKHURST, clad
> in his robe and slippers, ENTERS
> from the stairway.)

PARKHURST

What is going on down here?
> (Spots POLICEMEN. Surprised)
Oh, my goodness - the police!

1ST POLICEMAN

Ah, Mr. Parkhurst, if I'm not mistaken; Mr.
Clarkton's butler.

PARKHURST

Why, yes, that's correct. How did you...?

1ST POLICEMAN
(Waves article)
There was a mention of you in this article about your
boss and this lovely mansion.

2ND POLICEMAN
These crooks read the article, too. That's why they
broke in tonight. But you can tell Mr. Clarkton
everything is all right. We caught them before they
could steal the Berican Collection.

PARKHURST
(Confused) The what?

2ND POLICEMAN
The Berican Collection. They talk about it in the
article.

PARKHURST
Mr. Clarkton has many valuable possessions, but I've
never heard of anything called the Berican Collection.

1ST POLICEMAN
Well, maybe he didn't tell you about it.

PARKHURST

(A bit miffed) Sir, a man has no secrets from his butler.

1ST POLICEMAN

Read it for yourself, then.
            (He shows the article to PARKHURST.)
See.
            (Points to a sentence and reads)
"Mr. J.P. Clarkton, who is well known for the Berican
Collection he owns,..."
            (PARKHURST starts laughing hysterically
            at this.)
And what is it you're finding so funny, if I may ask?

PARKHURST

(Pointing to article) This. There's a typographical
error in this article.
            (As he moves to closet door, upstage)
Mr. Clarkton doesn't own any "Berican" collection.
What he has is a...
            (Opens the closet door)
beer can collection!
            (The open closet reveals shelf upon
            shelf of different brightly-
            colored beer cans.)

BOOMER

You mean, we went through all this trouble for
beer cans?

1ST POLICEMAN

(To burglars) For sure, boys. And that's just where
you're all going to end up - in the can!
                    (Indicating with his gun that the
                    burglars should move out the door.)
All right, let's get a move on, then.
                    (The burglars move toward the door,
                    which the 2ND POLICEMAN has opened.)

MUGGSY

(Sighs) I wonder what color license plates we're
stamping out this year.

CURTAIN

Markets

Publishers' Guidlines

As I mentioned in chapter 13, the market for plays written specifically for amateurs to produce is not nearly as large as that for fiction and non-fiction prose. That's why the listings for each are as extensive as I have been able to make them, based on information supplied to me from each publisher on their current needs. In many cases, I have quoted as much information as I thought to be applicable to the type of work you will be producing from their published "Submission Guidelines" when they were supplied to me; however, I have not quoted any publishers' entire Submission Guidelines. For a greater understanding of what they are looking for, I suggest writing for the guidelines and requesting a copy of their current catalog. Always include a SASE for guidelines. Some publishers charge a small fee for a copy of their catalog. Inquire about this.

I have contacted each publisher listed herein, and each was kind enough to take the time to respond personally (I told you they were nice people!). I am pleased to be able to pass along the following information.

Please read each listing carefully and select the publishers you are considering submitting to accordingly.

Once again, please write for a copy of their current guidelines (some change from time to time) before submitting. Pay careful attention to their specific needs and requirements for submissions.

You will notice that I have included material not specifically addressed in this book, such as musicals, plays for the Christian market, community theatre market, contests, etc., because you may be inclined to submit work for these markets if your special talents lean toward writing these sorts of plays.

Baker's Plays
100 Chauncy Street
Boston, MA 02111-1783
Voice: (617) 482-1280
FAX: (617) 482-7613

Send manuscripts to the attention of Raymond Pape, Associate Editor. Publishes full-length plays, one-acts, family theatre plays. Has an open submissions policy, but queries are welcome. Response time: Scripts: three to four months, Queries: one to two weeks. Negotiated royalty contract, book royalty.

(The following is quoted from their Submission Guidelines): "We currently publish full-length plays, one-act plays, theatre texts and musicals. Our market consists of high school, university, community, children's, family and regional theaters.

"We have a separate division which publishes plays specifically for religious institutions. Manuscripts must be typed in the standard play format and be securely bound. We prefer to read plays which have been "production tested," but we maintain an open submission policy. Synopses and sample pages are also welcome. Playwrights should include a script history and reviews. When submitting a musical, include a cassette tape of all the songs which are in the script. Always include a SASE (with enough postage) in the event that your manuscript requires a safe return. Submissions without a SASE will not be returned. We are always interested in new and exciting work. We generally require three to four months to read and evaluate a manuscript. The ideal time to submit work is from September to April, as the editorial staff is busy with catalogue preparation during the summer months."

Baker's Plays High School Playwriting Contest
CC/0 Baker's Plays
100 Chauncy Street
Boston, MA 02111

This was a playwriting contest Baker held in 1997 for high school students. They may or may not make it an annual contest, but the information is still valuable. Contact Baker's to find out the latest status of the contest.

(The following is quoted from their Submission Guidelines): "Open to any high school student. Plays should be about the "high school experience," but may also be about any subject and of any length, so long as the play can be reasonably produced on the high school stage. Plays must be accompanied by the signature of a sponsoring high school Drama or English teacher, and *it is recommended that the play receive a production or a public reading prior to submission.* Multiple submission and co-authored scripts are welcomed. Teachers may not submit a student's work. The manuscript must be firmly bound, typed and come with a self-addressed, stamped envelope. Include enough postage to cover the return of the manuscript. Plays that do not come with a SASE will not be returned. Do not send originals; copies only. All plays must be postmarked by January 31st of each year. Plays postmarked after this date will not be considered. Playwrights will be notified during the month of May. Awards are based on merit, and if no submission warrants an award, no prizes will be given."

"*Awards:* First place: $500.00 and the play will be published by Baker's Plays. Second Place: $250.00 and an Honorable Mention. Third Place: $100.00 and an Honorable Mention."

Eldridge Publishing Company, Inc.
Susan Shore, Editor
PO Box 1595
Venice, FL 34284
1-800-HI-STAGE

General Market: *(The following is quoted from their Submission Guidelines):*

"Eldridge Publishing is always looking for new plays. Please submit plays and musicals suitable for performance by community theatres and junior and senior high schools. For musical submissions, be sure to include a cassette tape of the music and lyrics and a sample of the printed score. We like all kinds of plays and are always open to new ideas. Generally speaking, our customers like plays with more female than male roles or flexible casting in which roles can be played by either men or women. This is not a hard and fast rule, however.

"We strongly recommend having your script workshopped, read or performed. We find scripts rewritten after this process are of a much higher caliber.

"We appreciate a cover letter giving us a brief description of the story of the play, its performance history, and if it has earned any awards. In addition, we would like to know a little about your writing experience.

"Also, please tell us...if you have included a stamped postcard for us to return immediately to acknowledge receipt of your script.

"We receive hundreds of manuscripts a year and want to give each careful attention and review. That's why it takes us about 2 months to respond. Be sure to include a SASE...so if we can't use your play you can continue to market it."

Christian Market: Address plays for the Christian market to Dorothy Dunham, Editor. *(The following is quoted from their Submission Guidelines):*

"Eldridge Publishing is always looking for new plays

and dedicated playwrights. In business since 1906, we are an independent publisher not supported by any denomination. We pride ourselves on dramas which will appeal to all Christians and hope our plays help spread the Word no matter what religion or size church.

"We publish about 25 new Christian plays a year. Generally we offer an outright purchase contract (from $100 to $500) with payment made upon publication.

"In full length plays (an hour or longer) we prefer large casts, about 10 characters or more. Flexible casting, that is roles which can be played by men or women are a real plus. Otherwise, we generally need more female roles than male. Skits and one-acts (about 30 minutes or less) may have smaller casts. We like easy costuming and scenery, if possible, as many church budgets are limited."

Grimpenmire Press
162 N. 17th Street
Springfield, OR 97477
Attn: Toni
Grimpenmir@aol.com

Uses both one-act and three-act plays, "but full lengths are easier to sell." No special cast requirements. "Prefer not to read plays that are written for shock value or contain gratuitous strong language. Plays sell better when they appeal to a broad spectrum."

Target audience is community theatre. Royalty contracts offered. "Our scripts are varied: mysteries (interactive and not), comedies, dramas, family-oriented, and one-acts."

"We try to read a manuscript within a month of receiving it, and most of the time we have no problem achieving this. For publication, anywhere between 3 to 12 months, depending on how busy we are and if electronic copies are available.

"We like to receive a query letter and detailed synopsis of the play (this can be e-mailed). Upon acceptance at this level, the manuscript may be submitted either by snail mail[1] or as an attached text file by e-mail. If the manuscript is submitted by snail mail and it is accepted, we request that an electronic copy be made available, or if we must have it keyed in, we do charge a reasonable fee (pro-rated to the length of the work)."

---

1. Snail mail is cyber-slang for mail sent through the postal system. - FVP

Heuer Publishing Company
Attn: C. Emmett McMullen, Editor
P.O. Drawer 248
Cedar Rapids, IA 52406
Editorial Line: (319) 364-6311
FAX (319) 364-1771
E-mail: hitplays@netins.net

(The following is quoted from their Submission Guidelines): "We sell exclusively to middle, junior and smaller senior high schools. Since the vast majority of people who perform our plays have little or no theatrical experience, simplicity and ease of production are chief factors in the acceptance of a play. We need plays with large, predominantly female casts. Please avoid controversial/offensive subject matter.

"We are primarily interested in full length comedies, farces, and mysteries, but we thoroughly enjoy reviewing well-developed one acts.

"We purchase the amateur rights and copyright the play in the author's name. The author retains all professional stage rights and all other professional rights.

"We are not responsible for manuscripts submitted without a self-addressed stamped envelope. Insured or registered mail submissions will not be accepted. Response time: two months."

Meriwether Publishing, Ltd.
Contemporary Drama Service
885 Elkton Drive
Colorado Springs, CO 80907
(For Church submissions) ATTN: Ms. Rhonda Wray
(For School Submission) ATTN: Mr. Theodore Zapel

Full manuscripts or queries. Looking for both one-act and full-length plays. Reporting time differs from play to play. Purchases outright, but occasionally offers royalty contracts. Rights purchased differ from author to author. Looking for material suitable for high school and community theatre performance.

(The following is quoted from their Guidelines for School Submissions): "Our primary markets are middle grades, junior highs, high schools, and some colleges. We are publishing nothing for the elementary level at present except for Sunday School plays for churches.

"Please include cast list, and (if required) prop list, costume information, set specifications, etc. with all play manuscripts. Following are the types of drama we publish:

· One-act non-royalty plays—originals or adaptations, comedies, parodies, social commentary and novelty drama. Plays with large and small casts and with many parts for women and a few plays for children's theatre.

· Speech contest materials—monologs for women and men, duologs, short playlets addressing the high school experience with honest feelings and real situations of current importance.

· Full-length plays—up to three acts, comedy, large casts.

· Adaptations—Shakespeare, the classics, and popular modern works (with original author permission).

· Oral interpretation—folktales and storytelling.

· Prevention plays—drama as a teaching tool about drug abuse, pregnancy, gangs, etc.

· Reader's theatre—adaptations or originals.

Query Letter Specifications:

· Include a synopsis or brief statement of objectives.

· Tell us why you believe your work deserves publication. Define the market you see as the potential audience.

· Please include a list of your publishing credits and/or experience and your payment expectations.

· Include a self-addressed, stamped envelope for our response.

Payment Terms:

·We normally purchase all rights. Sometimes we make anoutright purchase of a manuscript, but our usual practice is to offer a royalty contract with payments to an agreed purchase price. Rates vary according to work and credits of author/playwright. Special projects are negotiable."

(The following is quoted from their Guidelines for Church Submissions [Query letter specifications are the same as for School Submissions]):

"Following are the types of Drama we publish:

·One-act non-royalty plays on religious themes up to 20 pages.

·Christmas and Easter chancel drama or liturgy—length 30 minutes maximum—for children's Sunday School departments and also for adults.

· Collections of short sketches on a central theme—five per collection—humorous, entertaining, Christian.

· Religious musicals for Christmas and Easter—one hour maximum. (Computer-generated musical accompaniment score and cassette of performance preferred.)

Payment Terms:

"Contract offers vary according to market potential of the work. We purchase limited or total rights or offer a royalty contract of 10% of sales. We offer some royalty contracts with payment to an agreed purchase price. Rates vary according to script and credits of author/playwright. Special projects are negotiable."

New Plays Incorporated
Box 5074
Charlottesville, VA 22905
ATTN: Patricia Whitton, Publisher

"New Plays Incorporated specializes in plays for young audiences (mostly preschool through middle school, a little high school) to be performed by adults or teenagers. Full length in this field means somewhere between 50 minutes and an hour and fifteen minutes, usually. Manuscripts should have been successfully produced, directed by someone other than the author. Reporting time is usually two months, sometimes longer. Our contract with authors is that the author retains copyright and we act as agent for the play, taking a percentage of the royalty. It's worthwhile querying, especially if it's a name title (for instance, we already have a *Prince and the Pauper* adaptation and wouldn't be interested in another)."

IRT
73 Furby Street
Winnipeg, MB
Canada R3C 2A2
Voice: (204) 775-2923
FAX: (204) 775-2947
E-mail: atwood@blizzard.mb.ca
ATTN: IRT Acquisitions

Uses manuscripts that are full-length, one-act and 10 minute (or shorter) plays. Reporting time is four months approximately. Buys amateur rights, but will handle professional rights if requested. Accepts plays from any genre and for any audience level; however, plays for children and young adult audiences will be given first consideration at this time.

"Only official IRT submissions will be considered. Please contact us to request a submission package either by writing to the address above, phoning, faxing or by e-mail. Please include your regular mailing address (snail mail) in your request.

"IRT is a publish-on-demand service, meaning that accepted plays are described in a catalogue, but are not published unless they are ordered. There is no fee to join this service and, likewise, no advances paid to the writers. Writers receive standard royalties on plays sold."

Plays, The Drama Magazine For Young People
120 Boylston Street
Boston, MA 02116
Elizabeth Preston, Managing Editor

One Act Plays only. Prefers full manuscript. Purchases all rights, outright purchase. High school, middle and lower grades. Reports in 2-3 weeks. Note: *Plays, The Drama Magazine For Young People* prefers to have manuscripts formatted somewhat differently than the manner described in Chapter 12. Please send for their tip sheet, which includes a sample manuscript page format, before submitting to them.

(The following is quoted from their manuscript specifications sheet:) "*Plays, The Drama Magazine For Young People*, publishes approximately 75 wholesome, one-act plays each year (in seven issues, October through May, with a combined issue for January/February). We are in the market for good scripts to be performed by young people in junior and senior high, middle grades, and lower grades. Of particular interest are comedies, farces, dramas, mysteries and melodramas for year-round use, as well as plays for such holidays and special occasions as Halloween, Book Week, Black History Month, Thanksgiving, Valentine's Day, Mother's Day, Washington's Birthday, etc. *We use only secular plays for Christmas and other religious holidays.*

"In addition, we are looking for plays addressing environmental and human rights issues; historical plays; biographical sketches; fairy tales and folk tales; skits; monologues; puppet plays; creative dramatics programs; and dramatized classics. (Query first for dramatized classics, stories adapted must be in the public domain.) *We publish no music or musicals*, but plays may include original words to be sung to familiar tunes.

"Plays must be simple to produce, with minimum requirements for costumes, stage sets and lighting. One setting is preferred, and when more than one is required, the scene changes should be kept to a minimum.

"Payment for all manuscripts is made on acceptance.

Rates vary, according to the length of the play and age level for which it is appropriate. The magazine buys all rights.

"All submissions must be accompanied by a self-addressed envelope, large enough and with sufficient postage for the manuscript's return. Always keep a copy of your manuscript. If you do not wish the manuscript returned, enclose first-class SASE for editorial reply."

Players Press, Inc.
PO Box 1344
Studio City, CA 91614
ATTN: Editorials

Publishes one-act and full-length plays. Manuscripts or queries. Reporting time: queries—2 weeks; manuscripts—3 months to 12 months. Offers royalty contracts. Prefers to purchase all rights. Publishes all types of plays from preschool through professional, including classic theatre.

Samuel French, Inc.
45 West 25th Street
New York, NY 10010
ATTN: Editorial Department

Preference is for full manuscripts of one-act and full-length plays. Turnaround time is approximately 14 to 16 weeks.

Pioneer Drama Service, Inc.
PO Box 4267
Englewood, CO 80155-4267

"We generally respond to query letters within two weeks, and to scripts within three months. We prefer queries first, although we will accept unsolicited manuscripts. If an author wishes to send a manuscript without first querying, we strongly recommend that he or she is familiar with what we publish before doing so. We get a great many submissions that are simply not right for our company. The reporting time does depend on the season, with September, October, January and February being our busiest months. We offer royalty contracts and purchase all rights.

"We publish a wide variety of plays and musicals — full-length plays, musicals, children's theatre, melodramas, one-acts, and adaptations. We have recently developed a Social Awareness section that focuses on helping children, teens and young adults deal with such things as drugs, alcohol, and peer pressure. Our market is mostly comprised of schools, from elementary to high school. We do, however, also sell to children's theatre groups and community theatre groups as well."

Pioneer Drama Service also conducts a yearly play writing contest. Write to them for details.

Dramatic Publishing
Sara Clark, Editor
311 Washington Street, Box 129
Woodstock, IL 60098
Voice: (815) 338-7170
FAX: (815) 338-8981
E-Mail 75712.3621@compuserve.com

Looking for full-length plays, one-act plays and musicals. Reporting time is 14-18 weeks. Royalty contract offered. Purchases amateur and stock rights. Looking for all types of material, including plays for middle school, high school, senior adult theatre, and community theatre. Send full manuscript, rather than queries, along with reviews, production history, and a SASE.

I. E. Clark Publications
PO Box 246
Schulenburg, TX 78956-0246
ATTN: Donna Cozzaglio, Editorial Department

Publishes both one-acts and full-length plays. Reporting time: 2 months or more. Pays book and performance royalty. Buys all rights. Send either manuscript or query. Be sure to include SASE if material is to be returned. A good videotape of a performance is also desirable. Full writer's guidelines available on request (enclosed #10 SASE).

"We publish plays for all theatres. However, we almost never publish a play that has never been produced, preferably with a director other than the author. Please enclose newspaper reviews or other proofs of performance."

Index

Writers!

Do You Want More Info About Publishers And Editors?

The *Out-To-Lunch Market Report* is a bimonthly newsletter that tells you what's selling now!

• What's happening today in the publishing industry • What is selling in bookstores • What the editors are looking for now • Hard facts about contracts • The impact of literary legal cases • Which publishers are doing what kinds of books • The magazine markets • What movie and television producers want • Trends in Publishing • Inside gossip • Tips on submitting and selling your work • Genres • Conventions • Commentary and opinion

The *Out-To-Lunch Market Report* is compiled by Sharon Jarvis, a literary agent, editor, packager, publisher, and author with 28 years experience—and a former acquistions editor at Doubleday, Ballantine, Ace, Playboy and Popular Library. She is the author of 9 published books, fiction and non-fiction. As an agent she has sold hundreds of books of all types, both here and abroad. Her multimedia corporation, Toad Hall, Inc., also publishes fiction and non-fiction under numerous imprints.

Acknowledgments: Cover design and interior pages by Steven Dale. This book was designed on a Macintosh™ Quadra 630, using a UMAX™ Vista S8 scanner; Iomega ZIP and DELTIS™ Olympus external optical drives. All graphics were manipulated in ADOBE™ Photoshop, Text and page layout was done in PageMaker™. Body copy is New Century Schoolbook, display fonts are Corvinus Skyline and Techno Bold. 3-D cover and theme art elements were rendered in Ray Dream Designer™.

Steven's print media services can be reached at:
Steven Dale
23420 Happy Valley Dr.
Newhall CA 91321
FAX: 805 288-1754
E-mail: dale1der@ecom.net